Twayne's English Authors Series

Sylvia E. Bowman, *Editor*

INDIANA UNIVERSITY

Horace Walpole

Horace Walpole

By MARTIN KALLICH
Northern Illinois University

Twayne Publishers, Inc.   : :   New York

PR
3757
W2
Z68

PREFACE

This critical-analytical study of Horace Walpole surveys his enduring intellectual achievement as it is reflected in his major works. The minutiae of eighteenth-century social life, for which Walpole as a gossipy letter writer is the chief primary source of information, have generally been underplayed or avoided. Instead, emphasis has been placed on Walpole's varied literary output—his criticism, imaginative creations, and political memoirs, all those writings that have significantly contributed to his lasting reputation; and his letters are used whenever they may help illuminate these texts under discussion. Such an approach offers two advantages: first, it permits Walpole to be treated with the dignity that any serious and influential writer deserves; second, it reveals him in a refreshingly new light as a man with the capacity for sustained thought. This critical study, then, may be considered an introduction to a very important side of Walpole that has been underestimated or neglected—his thought—thereby providing the basis for further systematic analysis in depth.

Each section of each chapter, except for the first and the last, discusses one important publication in the Walpole canon. The section on Walpole's life includes a brief account of Walpole's major poetry. The Selected Bibliography lists the important works by and about Walpole; however, some titles have been included, even though they have contributed little or nothing directly to the results of this study. The first collected edition, *The Works of Horatio Walpole, Earl of Orford* (London, 1798), in five volumes, prepared by Walpole's friend, Mary Berry, supplies the basic texts discussed in this book, exclusive of the political memoirs and letters. The letters, which are referred to by date and the name of the person to whom they were addressed, can readily be found in the two best editions, as indicated in the bibliography, that by Mrs. Paget Toynbee (supplemented with three additional volumes by her husband) and that by Wilmarth S. Lewis, the Yale Walpole, which, when completed, will become standard and definitive. As yet there is no satisfactory edition of the memoirs—a work that challenges future scholarship.

I wish to acknowledge a debt of gratitude to Mrs. Betsy Harfst for reading, checking, and correcting my manuscript and for allowing me to include in abbreviated form an account of her intriguing psychoanalytic insights into *The Castle of Otranto* and *The Mysterious Mother* and to the editor of *Papers on Language and Literature* for permission to use in this book my article "Houghton Hall: The House of Walpole" (Fall, 1968). Everyone reading Walpole is, of course, indebted to W. S. Lewis and his associates for making available accurate texts of Walpole's letters and other writings and for painstakingly providing copious illuminating annotations indispensable for an understanding of a prolific, versatile, and enormously gifted writer.

MARTIN KALLICH
Northern Illinois University

CONTENTS

CHRONOLOGY

1717 September 24 (Old Style), Horace Walpole is born in London.

1727 April 26, goes to Eton.

1735 March 11, enters Cambridge University; Walpole at King's College, Thomas Gray at Peterhouse.

1737 August 20, mother dies.

1738 February, "Verses in Memory of King Henry VI: the Founder of King's College, Cambridge."

Summer, reaches his majority and is appointed to lucrative patent places, sinecures, which provide Walpole with his income throughout his life.

1739 March 10, leaves on Grand Tour with Gray; begins writing his famous letters.

1740 Writes "An Epistle to Mr. Ashton from Florence."

1741 May, quarrel with Gray begins; each returns separately.

September 12, lands at Dover on return from tour.

1742 Member of Parliament for the Borough of Callington, Cornwall (until 1754).

February, father resigns as first lord of the treasury, the chief minister, and is created earl of Orford.

March 23, Walpole's first speech in the House of Commons, one in defense of his father.

1745 November, reconciliation with Gray. Their friendship is uninterrupted until Gray's death in 1771.

March 18, father dies.

1747 May, leases a building at Strawberry Hill, near Twickenham; buys it in June, 1749.

Aedes Walpolianae: or a Description of the Collection of Pictures at Houghton Hall in Norfolk (Dedication dated from Houghton, 1743).

1751 Walpole begins to write his political *Memoirs*.

1753 February to September, 1756, occasional contributions, nine altogether, to *The World*.

1754 April 20, member of Parliament for Castle Rising, Norfolk.

1757 February, vacates seat for Castle Rising in order to be chosen for King's Lynn. Tries to save Admiral Byng.

May, *A Letter from Xo Ho.*
June, founds a printing press at Strawberry Hill.
1758 April, *A Catalogue of the Royal and Noble Authors of England.* Printed at Strawberry Hill.
Summer, *Fugitive Pieces in Verse and Prose.* Printed at Strawberry Hill.
1762 *Anecdotes of Painting in England* (completed in 1771).
1764 *The Castle of Otranto.*
1765 August, leaves for France, meets Mme du Deffand in Paris. (Visits Paris in 1767, 1769, 1771, 1775.)
1768 Last year in Parliament.
February, *Historic Doubts on the Life and Reign of King Richard III.*
March, completes *The Mysterious Mother.* Printed at Strawberry Hill.
1771 *The History of the Modern Taste in Gardening.*
1774 *A Description of the Villa of Horace Walpole at Strawberry Hill* (enlarged in 1784 and 1786).
1785 *Hieroglyphic Tales.* Printed at Strawberry Hill.
1791 Becomes the fourth Lord Orford upon death of nephew.
1797 March 2, dies. Interred at Houghton, Norfolk.

CHAPTER 1

The Man

I   *The Stereotype and the Reality*

IN A letter to Horace Mann (February 25, 1750), Horace Walpole, a member of Parliament and the wealthy son of the famous Prime Minister Sir Robert Walpole, expressed his opposition to the English slave trade, among the first of his age to disapprove of slavery on moral grounds:

We have been sitting this fortnight on the African Company: *we,* the British Senate, that temple of liberty, and bulwark of Protestant Christianity, have this fortnight been pondering methods to make more effectual that horrid traffic of selling negroes. It has appeared to us that six-and-forty thousand of these wretches are sold every year to our plantations alone!—it chills one's blood. I would not have to say that I voted in it for the continent of America! . . . We reproach Spain, and yet do not even pretend the nonsense of butchering these poor creatures for the good of their souls!

He frankly sympathized with the American struggle against oppression during the Revolutionary War, but the system of slavery in America was quite another matter: "If all the black slaves were in rebellion, I should have no doubt in choosing my side, but I scarce wish perfect freedom to merchants who are the bloodiest of tyrants. I should think the souls of the Africans would sit heavy on the swords of the Americans" (to Mason, February 14, 1774). We surely cannot think of a man who takes such a forthright stand as a hard-hearted aristocrat; his negative vote on slavery is evidence of his humanity. True, he may in some of his letters give the impression of a man of fashion, easily bored, detached, disillusioned, cynical. But evidences in other letters of an undetached and uncynical charity, if not ostentatious or sensational, are also in clear conflict with this well-known stereotype of Walpole.

1

For example, to choose at random from his letters, he also offered money to the distressed, to the subscription for French prisoners in England during the Seven Years' War, and to the sick prisoners in the Southwark and Marshalsea jails (to Bedford, September 24, 1762; February 29, 1764). Furthermore, he had painfully humane and unpatriotic qualms about victories in war, for the cost to human life appalled him (to Mann, October 3, 1762). He was angered by the monstrous iniquities of the English East India Company (to Mann, November 4, 1772), and he admitted that in India "we beat . . . Spain in avarice and cruelty" (to Mann, April 9, 1772). He also had very close friends who could supply additional evidence of his tender warmth and generosity; for example, Henry Conway, to whom he once offered practically the whole of his fortune (July 20, 1744). His moral commitment to life, as suggested by his humane behavior, is a very real part of the man, and sometimes it was expressed with great intensity.[1] By his own declaration, he wanted his real friends to know that under the veneer of detachment there were "some very serious qualities, such as warmth, gratitude, and sincerity" (to Lady Hervey, January 12, 1760).

Another stereotype of Walpole presents him as an effeminate, glittering man of the world, eager to attend parties of the elite at their rendezvous, Vauxhall or Ranelagh; to gamble (but not quite so recklessly) at White's or Almack's; or to play whist, loo, faro, or cribbage with malicious old dowagers and to enjoy with them spicy morsels of scandalous gossip about several varieties of extra-marital affairs or about young heiresses eloping with their footmen. This is the image of a social butterfly with nothing more important to do than flit from one party to another and fill with the usual party trivialities the enormous void of a leisurely existence. Walpole himself suggests the truth of this picture because he was very sociable and did love parties, as he confesses in numerous letters—about as much as he loved solitude. He made no claim to learning, paraded his negligence, often betrayed an aversion to any suspicion of professionalism until these affectations became habitual. Thus at the age of seventy-two, when he summed up his career to John Pinkerton, he referred in a self-deprecating way to his "inferior" understanding, "incapable of sound, deep application"; and he described his pursuits as "light and trifling, [tending] to nothing but casual amusement," and his studies and productions as "desultory" (August 19, 1789). Thus Walpole modestly underrates his own performance, encouraging a severe judgment on a fribble.

Such is the stuff from which Thomas Macaulay could easily have concocted his abusive estimate of Walpole's character and total achievement.[2] Seizing upon the "glaring faults of Horace Walpole's head and heart," Macaulay infers that "none but an unhealthy and disorganized mind could have produced such literary luxuries" as his curious works. He sees Walpole as the "most eccentric, the most fastidious, the most capricious of men," full of whimsies and affectations; an unconscious hypocrite whose behavior was consistently at variance with his pretensions (concerning philanthropy, the court and society, literary fame); a conscious hypocrite in his affectation of liberty (really Whig cant, the implications of which were beyond his comprehension) and of republican principles (which his activity as a courtier obviously contradicted); a comical fool seriously obsessed with trifles; a scandalmonger who confused gossip with politics; an aristocrat "who never for a moment forgot that he was an Honourable." In short, to Macaulay, Walpole was insincere—or, what is worse, incapable of sincerity; odd and incompetent; a poor judge of character "who sneered at everybody" and whose opinions about men and things, "wild, absurd, and ever-changing," were almost worthless. Macaulay's polemic, written in beautifully limpid prose, is cruelly destructive. But it is obviously unjust, and many of the supposed statements of fact on which the judgment is based are simply untrue.

All stereotypes are reductive caricatures, and all satires necessarily simplify, dehumanize, and distort—even those that originate in an ironic and diffident self. The real Walpole is hardly recognizable in Macaulay's classic essay on an eccentric fop and conceited fool, or in the self-portrait by a retired old gentleman approaching death. We can scarcely tell from Macaulay's extravagant or Walpole's sentimental misrepresentation that this person was once young and energetic, industrious and creative, complex and ambivalent—a pioneer in art, perhaps not a profound thinker or "a great reasoner," as Macaulay with his superior air complains, but certainly a very influential man of taste. Yet even Macaulay admits that in some strange way Walpole's mind was somehow fascinating and that his writings possessed "irresistible charm," were never dull but always entertaining—if only "baubles."

In this study an attempt is made to present a side of this eighteenth-century celebrity that has been neglected much too long because of a kind of inverted snobbery, a blinding prejudice against one who, as Lord Byron has said in his preface to *Marino Faliero* (1821), is accused simply of being a gentleman and a nobleman. It cannot be denied, of course, that Walpole was a man of wealth and high social position; but, at the same time, he was by no means a mere dabbler in literature and the arts, as he often affects to describe himself. He had the capacity to think; and his thought, because it was taken seriously in his lifetime, deserves serious consideration in ours. Admittedly important for his many contributions to history, literature, and art, he requires careful attention so that he can be understood in his true complexity as a thinking human being charged with deep and genuine feelings. In this study, then, the temptation to listen to his gossip will be suppressed; and, undistracted by trivia, we will be free to deal with the life of the mind, the large principles and major themes structuring whatever in Walpole's thought can be considered intellectually significant.

That Walpole was an aristocrat who shared the taste and point of view of his class is quite true. However, this reductive cliché is almost meaningless, for it obscures the real problem of criticism: to define the nature and quality of Walpole's aristocratic point of view and his achievement as a unique individual despite handicaps of class conditioning. As an example of this critical problem, we may ask if there is any ambivalence in the way Walpole unconsciously uses in his novel *The Castle of Otranto* the romantic fairy-tale motif of the changeling poor boy who is really of the true nobility as proved by a strawberry birthmark. As another illustration of this problem, we have the following apparently trivial detail: Walpole, when taken to task by David Hume for his critical treatment of Sir Philip Sidney in his *Catalogue of Royal and Noble Authors,* answered in self-defense: "To say the truth, I attribute the great admiration of Sir Philip Sidney to his having so much merit and learning for a man of his rank" (July 15, 1758). That last phrase, "of his rank," is a significant qualification which suggests Walpole's real attitude to the shallow amateurs of high society. True, he often praised them unduly, but many of them were his friends and to do otherwise would have been bad policy and worse manners. Still, a phrase like this one about Sidney provides a clue to his honest opinion.

The same can be said about his political views. He did not agree with members of his class, the ruling class, on all issues; and in declarations of his political creed, he often took a stand against aristocratic government. Nor should his opposition to the French Revolution be considered clear evidence of inconsistency caused merely by aristocratic prejudices, although certainly in this instance the force of such prejudices should not be underestimated. He certainly did not object to the demolition of the Bastille; he wrote to Hannah More in September, 1789, that he "always hated to drive by it knowing the miseries it contained." He admired, he wrote to Lady Ossory on August 22, 1791, "with Mr. Charles Fox . . . the destruction of despotism"; but he agreed with Mr. Burke in abhorring "the violence, cruelty, injustice, and absurdity of the National Assembly." To him, the French National Assembly represented the tyranny of the *many* (to Miss Berry, April 3, 1791; to Lady Ossory, October 13, 1789)—and tyranny from whatever quarter, because dependent on oppressive force and violence, he consistently and unequivocally rejected. The French, he declared to Conway in July, 1790, acted "frantically," hysterically; the Americans, "rationally."

His attitude toward religion offers an interesting problem. He noted in a letter to Mann on February 7, 1772, the failure to have Parliament abolish or revise the Thirty-nine Articles of the Episcopal Confession, which he described as "that summary of impertinent folly . . . so much more difficult is it to expel nonsense than sense—for sense makes few martyrs." He rejected the possibility or expediency of orthodoxy in religion. To his friend the Reverend William Cole, who was extremely High Church, he declared that he wished to concentrate on essentials in religion—a belief in God and an ethical code; he could not accept the Thirty-nine Articles because to do so meant limiting his faith—and that he refused to define narrowly. Thus he rejected—again to Cole, who must have read these words with pain and chagrin—ecclesiastical pretensions as well as the theology that buttressed them: "Exalted notions of church matters are contradictions in terms to the lowliness and humility of the Gospel. There is nothing sublime but the Divinity. Nothing sacred but His work" (July 12, 1778).

These comments match Walpole's consistent attacks on Roman Catholicism, which thread through the works of his lifetime, for its bigotry and superstition. He admitted (to Mann on November 8, 1784), that he has "ever been averse to toleration of an intolerant religion." But the fundamental point at issue should not be overlooked. As the context of this last letter demonstrates, it was the violent suppression of human freedom by a militant church that made him feel this way. Thus, to cite another example, he gave a negative to the anti-Catholic Gordon riots, for he wrote to Mann on June 4, 1780, "I abhor such Protestantism as breathes the soul of Popery, and commences a reformation by attempting a massacre." These are almost the same words he was to use to Lady Ossory on August 4, 1789, about the French Revolution: "I still less like liberty displayed by massacre, and without legal trials." In matters of religious belief, if we may hazard a conclusion, Walpole was deistical, humanely open-minded, frankly unorthodox, and by no means a conservative Tory; and, lastly, he was as libertarian as he professed to be in politics.

Helped by such clues as these, ambiguous *or* clear, we can enrich our picture of Walpole and see him in depth as a very engaging personality responding with intelligence and with some consistency to the alternatives that his life and times presented to him. From the moral point of view, some of his responses, as already indicated, were remarkable; from the esthetic point of view, some of his achievements were no less so.

Walpole's literary reputation rests principally on his letters published after his death. Today we think letters are ephemeral—but not Walpole in the eighteenth century. Like many writers of his time, he valued letters as literature and took care that most of them would be carefully preserved. Some are highly polished compositions, elaborate and great set pieces—like the letters about the trial and execution of the rebel Scottish lords (to Mann, August 1, 1746; August 21, 1746); the entertainments at Vauxhall (to Montagu, June 23, 1750); the birthday ball for the Prince of Wales (to the earl of Strafford, June 7, 1760); the funeral of George II (to Montagu, November 13, 1760); the coronation of George III (to Montagu, September 24, 1761; to Mann, September 28, 1761); the decline of Houghton (to Montagu, March 25, 1761); the house party at Stowe (to Montagu, July 7, 1770). But, for the most part, the letters reveal Walpole as master of the light touch, as, for example, when in a letter to Montagu on August 12, 1760, he describes himself suffering from the gout—"Ariel the sprite in a slit toe." He was not indifferent to great things, but his forte lay in exhibiting the greatness of little things—domestic items, traits of individual character, anecdotes of people, "a thousand trifles and negligences, which give grace, ease, and familiarity to correspondence" (to the earl of Strafford, December 11, 1783).

At present, there are about six thousand known letters in the Walpole correspondence, extending over sixty years, and about four thousand by Walpole himself. As a result of this enormous amount of writing, we have a vivid, authentic record by a responsive spectator of eighteenth-century culture. If only because of his indefatigable industry as a correspondent, and his talent for elegance and for maintaining an air of immediacy and spontaneity, Walpole should be considered important as a prose stylist and as the social historian of his time—the chief source of knowledge of life in eighteenth-century England.[3] He thought of himself as the chronicler of his time, an informal "gazetteer" who was writing for posterity. He became one of the greatest English letter writers.

But it must not be forgotten that Walpole was a man of letters as well as a letter writer. This other side of Walpole's versatile genius is examined in this study, with illustrations and supporting details taken from the letters. Walpole tried all forms of writing—verse, satiric and political pamphlets, periodical essays, *catalogues raisonnées*, political history, literary history, art history, biography, memoirs, the novel, the tale, and the drama. He pioneered in imaginative literature with his Gothic romance, *The Castle of Otranto,* and with his Gothic drama, *The Mysterious Mother;* in literary history with his *Catalogue of Royal and Noble Authors,* popular for about a century after its first publication; in art history with his *Anecdotes of Painting,* still a standard source of information for art before 1750.

His political memoirs, at which he industriously labored, extend over forty years (from 1751 to 1791), thereby providing a lively commentary on parliamentary affairs and secret and intimate glimpses into political personalities and events that are of immeasurable value to the historian. Nor should his reputation as a connoisseur be overlooked. Walpole had a good deal to do with changing trends in taste by making Gothic architecture and the natural English garden fashionable. He wrote on these subjects and he put his ideas into practice by remodeling his country estate, building and grounds, at Strawberry Hill.

For all these reasons, there cannot be any question of his importance as an influential historian, learned art critic, sensitive and prolific writer, taste maker, and even thinker. Analysis of his achievement in all these areas of thought and taste helps us define accurately a substantial portion of the truth concerning the man and the reflective life to which he was genuinely committed.

II   *A Life Portrait*

Horatio Walpole, who was born September 24, 1717, was the third son and youngest child of Catherine Shorter and Sir Robert Walpole. His mother was the eldest daughter of John Shorter, a wealthy Baltic timber merchant; and her grandfather, Sir John, had been lord mayor of London under James II in 1688. John Dryden, Walpole says, was her great uncle;[4] and her sister was the mother of Walpole's most intimate relative and life-long friend, Henry Seymour Conway. Walpole's father, Sir Robert, the famous prime minister under the first two Georges, was noted for protecting the succession of the Hanoverian princes against the Jacobite Stuarts and for keeping his country at peace for twenty years, a remarkable achievement. Upon his retirement a few years before his death, Sir Robert was raised to the peerage as the first earl of Orford.

Horatio, or Horace (the name Walpole preferred because it appeared to be more suitable for an Englishman), was the last of six children—Robert, Junior, Mary, Edward, William (died in infancy), and Catherine (died at nineteen). Horace did not appear to have anything in common with his eldest brother Robert; but Edward, interestingly enough, had tastes like his own—he was an art patron (Louis François Roubiliac, the famous sculptor, was indebted to him) and a musician. He played on the violoncello and invented a stringed instrument which he called "the pentachord." Yet despite this affinity, a scandal based on the supposition that Horace had absolutely nothing in common with his brothers, in appearance as well as sensibility, was maliciously generated in the nineteenth century long after he had died. The source of this gossip was Lady Louisa Stuart; in her "Introductory Anecdotes" (1837) published in *The Letters and Works of Lady Mary Wortley Montagu,* she comments on the aversion that the Walpole and Montagu ladies had for each other, remarks Walpole's affection for his mother, and then declares that a scandalous side to her character was familiar to everyone but Horace: "In a word, Horace Walpole was generally supposed to be the son of Carr Lord Hervey, and Sir Robert not to be ignorant of it."[5]

The scandalous gossip is probably untrue. It is worth noting that Lady Louisa's remark, written in 1836, was based on what she remembered reading forty or fifty years earlier in the journals of her grandmother Lady Mary Wortley Montagu before they were destroyed by her mother Lady Bute. The story, coming over a long stretch of time and from a second-hand source, can scarcely be credited. Distortions could also be caused not only by faulty memory, but by partiality; for Lady Mary certainly favored her close friend, Robert Walpole's mistress, Maria Skerritt. This gossip must have had its real origin in the extramarital affairs of the notorious second Lady Orford, wife of Robert, Junior, and widespread rumors that the father of her son, the third earl, was Sir George Oxenden.[6] Lady Louisa's story is undoubtedly a garbled version of this affair dealing with the second generation of Robert Walpole's family.

Furthermore, there is no contemporary evidence to support Lady Louisa's statement, including testimony by Sir Robert himself. Nor is there any evidence of the father's neglect for any reason of his infant or young son. Apparently, no one in his lifetime doubted Horace's legitimacy. Not even Horace himself in all his voluminous writings had anything to say about it.[7] In his very first letter (1725), one addressed to his mother and written when he was eight years old, he exhibits a normal sentimental concern for his father ("I hop papa is wall . . . and pray give my Duty to papa."), thereby suggesting that their relationship was not unusually unpleasant or even negative.

At any rate, Walpole felt very close to his mother. When over seventy years of age, he writes very sentimentally about his relationship with her:

As I was the youngest by eleven years of Sir Robert Walpole's children by his first wife, and was extremely weak and delicate, as you see me still, though with no constitutional complaint till I had the gout after forty, and as my two sisters were consumptive and died of consumptions, the supposed necessary care of me (and I have overheard persons saying "That child cannot possibly live") so engrossed the attention of mother, that compassion and tenderness soon became extreme fondness.[8]

When he was about nine and a half years old, Walpole went to Eton (April 26, 1727). The following month he had a brief audience with King George I, which he fondly recorded in the first chapter of his *Reminiscences.* His father provided him with this very unusual opportunity to visit the king in his private apartment, for which there was no precedent—another indication that Sir Robert by no means neglected his young son, "a favorite child," as Walpole himself says. Furthermore, because his memory of this incident was so vivid after more than sixty years we can infer that it made a powerful impression on him and that he must have invested it with a good deal of psychological significance. Symbolically, it meant loyalty to the king and the Protestant succession, loyalty to his father because so closely associated with the king, and loyalty to the monarchy (for when he wrote the *Reminiscences* in 1788, it must be remembered that talk about republican leveling was fashionable). True, Walpole asserted more than once his criticism of monarchy; and he even declared in the same chapter of his *Reminiscences* that by 1742, when his father fell from the premiership, "I had lost all taste for courts and princes and power," [9] yet on the other hand his alleged republicanism surely could not have gone very deep in view of his early conditioning.

At Eton, Walpole, made many lasting friendships. His closest friends were divided into two groups—the "triumvirate" and "quadruple alliance." The first comprised George Montagu, who became an idle gentleman, and Charles Lyttelton, who became a clergyman with antiquarian tastes, and Walpole. Perhaps the other Montagu brother, Charles, later a lieutenant general and Knight of the Bath, was also associated with this group. Walpole carried on an extensive correspondence with George Montagu up to the year 1771; and in his oft-quoted letter to George of May 6, 1736, Walpole makes clear that at Eton he was by no means the rugged athletic type. We are led to picture a slight, effeminate, delicate young boy of refined sensibility.

But whatever love Walpole had for literature was cultivated by his relationship with the other less aristocratic but far more intellectual group which formed the "quadruple alliance." Walpole shared their literary interest in pastoral French romances and in English heroic drama. Thomas Gray, the most important figure of this literary circle, was thirteen years old—a little older than Walpole—and his mother kept a milliner's shop. However, Richard West, also a little older, was the son of the Irish lord chancellor and grandson of Bishop Burnet, whose *History of My Own Time* Walpole admired and to some extent tried to emulate in his *Memoirs.* The precocious poet of the group, West was already writing verses in Latin and English. West died in his twenties of consumption, but not before he received some wonderful letters from Walpole who was then touring Europe. Thomas Ashton's social origin was as humble as Gray's; his father was an usher in a grammar school at Lancaster, with a teacher's miserable income. Walpole addressed to Ashton his most important early work, the "Poetical Epistle" of 1740, written while on his travels; but toward the end of their relationship, about twenty years after Eton, Walpole had only contempt for him.

At Eton, Walpole made a few other lasting friends besides Montagu and Gray—George Augustus Selwyn, the celebrated gambler and wit; and William Cole, an antiquary with whom Walpole carried on an extensive correspondence. Lastly, another group of close friends must be mentioned, both first cousins to Walpole on the maternal side, Lord Conway (Francis Seymour, afterward Lord Hertford), and his younger brother Henry Seymour Conway. Walpole was closer to the younger Conway than to anyone else throughout their long lives. Their relationship was of immeasurable importance to Walpole.

Like Gray, who vividly described his strong sentimental feeling for Eton in his famous ode, Walpole had only "the most agreeable recollections" of his experience at school (to West, August 17, 1736). His taste for literature was formed at Eton; and his friendships made there were numerous and enduring, as proved by his extensive correspondence with his Eton comrades over the years. Harry Conway, his contemporary at Eton, was two years younger; and perhaps Walpole's profound concern for the younger boy, whom he always associated with his mother, was strengthened at school, thereby determining his own behavior in later years in more ways than he was himself aware.

On September 23, 1734, just before his seventeenth birthday, Walpole left Eton, and, after a brief interval of residence in London, went up to Cambridge University on March 11, 1735. The "quadruple alliance" had only partially disintegrated—West was at Oxford, but Ashton and Gray had already been almost a year at Cambridge—Ashton at Walpole's college, King's; and Gray at Peterhouse. Cole was also at Cambridge, and so most of Walpole's Eton friendships were continued. Henry Conway, however, did not enroll at either university.

Walpole remained at Cambridge for almost four years, but his periods of residence were irregular. He was instructed in law, anatomy, Italian, drawing, logic, philosophy, mathematics (in which he was a failure),[10] and the Classical languages (in which he was not particularly proficient). He did not care for the Cambridge curriculum that forced upon him subjects that he disliked, for he preferred literature and recent history. He deplored the stress on logic and abstruse philosophy, the neglect of "polite literature, and all knowledge of this world" (to West, August 17, 1736). However, because he did not have to take the curriculum seriously and was free to do as he pleased, he did not actively dislike Cambridge.

But the importance of the university to Walpole's formative years is indicated in the tremendous influence that one of the fellows, Conyers Middleton, had upon him. Middleton influenced his admiring young student, originally (as Walpole confesses in his *Memoirs*) of "a strong religious enthusiastic turn of mind," to shift "to the infidel side."[11] Middleton imbued his pupil with a fierce resentment against not only priests but kings, too—notions congenial to the mature Walpole, who was Whiggish and Deistic in his inclinations. These influences the soon-to-be-written verse "Epistle to Ashton" demonstrates. That Walpole venerated Middleton as his intellectual god and always thought of him with pleasure can be inferred from the fact that Middleton's portrait by John Giles Eckhardt hung in Walpole's bedchamber at Strawberry Hill.[12]

Except for one work, Walpole's literary production at Cambridge was negligible. With other young college poets he addressed congratulatory verses in Latin to the Prince of Wales upon his marriage in 1736; and on February 2, 1738, he dedicated a poem to the memory of Henry VI, founder of King's College. This second piece, one of his most ambitious flights, is noteworthy for two reasons: it expresses his obsessive hostility for Roman Catholic "superstition," and it anticipates his later commitment to the Gothic style. The poem begins with a resounding blast at Catholicism, "Superstitions's papal gloom":

> While Superstition teaches to revere
> The sainted Calendar and letter'd year;
> While Bigots joy in canonizing Shades,
> Fictitious Martyrs, visionary Maids. . . .

Walpole prefers the dignity and restraint of the English Episcopal service:

> Here mild Devotion bends her pious knee,
> Calm and unruffled as a summer sea;
> Avoids each wild enthusiastic tone,
> Nor borrows utt'rance from a tongue unknown.

He then proceeds to praise the charitable king and to celebrate his lovely Gothic chapel, the best "Monument to Henry's name," its "vaulted roofs" and "shooting columns." Young Walpole is certainly aware of the difference between neo-Classical and Gothic architectural styles; and he praises the chapel as the work of a genius who has not been subjected to regularizing rules:

> Art and Palladio had not reached the land,
> Nor methodiz'd the Vandal Builder's hand:
> Wonders, unknown to rule, these piles disclose:
> The Walls, as if by inspiration rose.

Beautiful King's College Chapel—its walls "Neat without art, and regularly plain," "the grandeur of the Gothic isle"—must have had a profound influence on the young man. These lines that express his pleasure in Gothic architecture demonstrate that Walpole at the early age of twenty-one already responded to romantic medievalism.

If, as Kenneth Clark suggests, the Gothic Revival was mainly literary in its inspiration, then these verses in praise of a Gothic structure—perhaps the first of their kind in the eighteenth century and far more significant than the mere Gothic allusions of David Mallet, Edward Young, and Robert Blair—may, as W. S. Lewis has written, "establish the claim that Walpole's was the main influence in the Gothic Revival. They are to poetry what Strawberry Hill is to domestic architecture and what *The Castle of Otranto* is to fiction."[13]

Walpole always felt deeply about King's College Chapel. For example, after a visit to Cambridge, he wrote to Cole on May 22, 1777, that the beauty of the building "penetrated" him "with a visionary longing to be a monk in it." The chapel fostered and formed his romantic attitude and fed his need for visions (to Montagu, January 5, 1766).

Walpole wrote verses throughout his life, but his poems are, as he described them, truly "fugitive," dashed off quickly and characteristically expressive of emotional detachment. Only at the beginning of his literary career did he think, although hesitantly, that he could aspire to poetry. In the poem about King's College Chapel and a few others that follow, he expressed himself with a certain degree of intensity and a sustained moral earnestness suggestive of emotional commitment; thereafter, the Muse trifled. In his maturity, he rarely wrote satire in verse, and never extensively; he never went beyond an occasional epigram, and, in his poetry, he was never introspective or analytical about his most deeply cherished ideas or about life and himself.

Personal anguish and anxiety simply cannot be found in his verse; for, after his early pieces, he never wrote under great internal pressure. All appears to be on the surface; he talks in verse, never sings. The verse reflects the same even and sprightly tone of the letters, detached, objective, gay, witty—and expresses similar social prejudices as it deals with the concerns of the well-to-do leisure aristocracy: gallant extempore compliments to young, beautiful ladies, invitations to old dowagers, epitaphs, riddles, and fantasies for the children of his friends. And all these rather hasty efforts are intended for casual amusement.

On the whole, Walpole's poetry shows him in what Macaulay has been pleased to consider his most accustomed garb, that of a trifler, the "trifler of the band," as the poet himself says in "The Parish Register." He belongs, as Pope has so aptly put it, to "the mob of Gentlemen who wrote with ease." As a matter of fact, he styled himself a gentleman author. Thus, his main object was to avoid pedantry and to appear elegant, or gracefully negligent. Although he did enjoy Milton's *Paradise Lost*, it seems as if Christopher Anstey's *New Bath Guide* gave him more pleasure because of its gossipy wit and sparkle—his chief requisites for poetry being wit, humor, and grace.[14]

Even as early as 1737 (to West, January 3, 1737) he expressed no confidence in his creative powers: "I assure you I don't think I am at all a Poet, but from loving Verses try to make some now and then: There are few but try in their lives, and most of us succeed alike." This confession introduces a poem that begins as follows:

> Seeds of Poetry and Rhime
>   Nature in my Soul implanted;
> But the Genial Hand of Time,
>   Still to ripen 'em is wanted;
> Or soon as they begin to blow
> My cold Soil nips the buds with Snow.[15]

The candor in the last line has biographical interest; for, at the age of twenty, in the image of inhibiting "cold soil," he recognizes his own limitations and confesses to failure in passion, a frigidity that, becoming habitual, developed into a permanent personality trait and affected his writings and even his personal relationships. But the fact that he admits he is not a poet indicates regret; and the fact that he saved his ephemera for posterity, that he could not bear to throw away any scrap of his own work, just as he projected himself into his huge collection of virtu, demonstrates a pathetic fear of losing his identity.

Before Walpole had completed his twentieth year, his mother died on August 20, 1737. A letter that he wrote to Charles Lyttelton on September 18, 1737, and another that Gray wrote to West on August 22, 1737, provide evidence of profound affection for her. He composed the eulogizing epitaph for her monument in Westminster Abbey. Apparently, he was the only one in the family who felt very deeply about Lady Walpole. Certainly, his father's grief was not lasting, for he married his mistress Maria Skerritt only six months later.

Approximately at the time he reached his majority, and not long after his mother's death, Walpole was blessed with several lucrative sinecures which gave him an income of over £2,000 a year for the rest of his life. His father also arranged that the Cornish pocket borough of Callington should return him to Parliament upon the first opportunity. As the third and youngest son, Walpole received the least from his father, who had purchased several patent places for his three sons. The eldest, Robert, held for life the office of Auditor of the Exchequer, valued, Horace himself said, at £8,000 a year, an enormous sinecure; Robert was also Master of the Fox Hounds, Ranger of Richmond New

Park, and Knight of the Bath.[16] Edward was Clerk of the Pells, an employment for life, which in the 1780's was valued at £7,000 a year and which Horace called "the second most valuable office in the Exchequer for life."[17] Besides, Edward held other offices also worth additional money, one of which Horace shared with him.

Around 1745 Horace's places as Usher of the Receipt of the Exchequer, Controller of the Great Roll, and Clerk of the Estreats brought him about £2,500 a year of unearned income—no mean sum at this time; and so he felt properly grateful for his portion, which, although much inferior to his brothers', "still it was a noble fortune for a third son and much beyond what I expected or deserved," as he himself admitted.[18] There is no doubt that Sir Robert was a considerate parent and father, who made sure that his three sons would be wealthy. Horace Walpole never really had to worry about money, although he at times did.

Thus although Walpole's income was modest in comparison with his brothers', it was ample enough to enable him to live at his own expense. The first thing he decided to do was to follow his brother Edward's example and make a gentleman's tour of the Continent. This trip, which lasted about two and a half years (March, 1739, to September, 1741), completed his education. In March, 1739, he left Cambridge without taking a degree and invited Gray to be his companion—Walpole was to pay all the expenses, but Gray was to be on terms of absolute equality and independence. They moved leisurely through the channel cities of Calais and Boulogne, and then rolled on to Amiens and St. Denis, eventually reaching Paris in early April, where they were greeted by the English residents, notably Walpole's cousins, the two Conways. In Paris, they dined with the English ambassador (the elder Conway), saw the ballet, went to the opera and theater, and enjoyed themselves sightseeing. They visited churches and palaces filled with pictures, including Versailles, whose architecture they disliked but whose artificial gardens gave them some pleasure.

In June, Henry Conway accompanied them to Rheims, where they remained for three months partying and learning the language. They went on an excursion to Geneva through the Savoy on purpose to see the Convent of the Grand Chartreuse in the mountains, and were thrilled by the romantic situation of the place. The letters of Walpole to West (September 28–October 2, 1739) and of Gray to his mother (November 16, 1739) describing this trip are well known. The gloomy chapel and the narrow cloisters, the uncouth but picturesque nature of its location, and the terrifying mountain scenery must have deeply affected Walpole and inspired the Gothic soul of the future author of *The Castle of Otranto*. But Walpole's reaction to the Grande Chartreuse is sensuous, visual, pictorial; he thinks of Salvator Rosa. Gray, on the other hand, is transcendental and spiritual as he writes of the mountain scenery "pregnant with religion and poetry." Nothing explains better the nature of these two young men than their different reactions to the scene.

Leaving Conway in Geneva, they traveled over the Alps, which terrified them, to Italy where they could "hate the foul monkhood" (to West, from Bologna, 1739). At Christmas, 1739, Walpole met Horace Mann in Florence. Mann's chief business as British envoy was to keep informed of Stuart movements in Rome and to report any evidences of Jacobite conspiracy to the government at home, a job that Walpole, as son of the chief minister, enjoyed contributing to as much as he could. In Florence, Gray studiously visited the art galleries, taking notes of pictures and statues, and forming a collection of manuscript music; but Walpole's enthusiasm for art had waned somewhat as he became more interested in society—in suppers, balls, masquerades, and carnivals. They also went to Rome, where youthful Horace had an opportunity to spy on the Pretender's sons and to report Stuart machinations to Mann in Florence.

On the way back home, a misunderstanding with Gray developed, which in later years Walpole explained in two letters to Gray's biographer, William Mason (March 2, 1773; November 27, 1773). However, the full explanation of the quarrel between the two, undoubtedly originating in personality differences, can never be given. But Walpole generously took the blame upon himself, admitting that he "was too young, too fond of . . . diversions . . . too much intoxicated by indulgence, vanity, and the insolence of my situation, as a Prime Minister's son, not to have been inattentive and insensible to the feelings of one I thought below me." This confession says plenty; indeed, it is surprising that Gray, who was morbid and very touchy about his independent and free spirit, and Walpole were ever close friends at all—before or after this event![19] They returned separately to England, Walpole arriving in England on September 12, 1741; Gray about two weeks before. The two effected a reconciliation in 1745; and from that time to Gray's death in 1771 their friendship was uninterrupted and was as warm as Gray wished to make it.

The Grand Tour had a profound and complicated meaning for Walpole. It gave him the friendship of Horace Mann, to whom he wrote copiously for almost half a century without ever seeing his correspondent again. In this, his longest correspondence, Walpole used Mann as an outlet for his social and political commentary. The tour also gave him the friendship of John Chute, who was to become a great help in designing Strawberry Hill. The tour gave Walpole his experience with new scenery—the rugged mountain scenery of the Alps in the Savoy, the Tuscany Hills, and the pastoral *campagna* around Rome—and with the landscape paintings of the great masters Salvator Rosa, Claude Lorrain, Gaspar Poussin. Ultimately, these experiences helped determine his expectations for art, for painting and garden design, in England. But it should be mentioned that he never again went in quest of romantic mountain scenery at home or abroad. He did not tour Scotland or the Lake District with Gray.

The Continental tour also broadened Walpole's cultural horizons in other ways. Although he was not quite so systematic as Gray in his search for art experiences, he absorbed a variety of cultural values, consciously or unconsciously. The architectural beauties, the many paintings, *objets d'art,* and antiquities that he saw in the famous galleries of Italy added to his already not so inconsiderable knowledge derived from his father's collection at Houghton. Apparently even his father trusted his taste and gave him commissions to purchase art treasures: "I am far gone in medals, lamps, idols, prints, etc., and all the small commodities to the purchase of which I can attain; I could buy the Colosseum, if I could" (to Conway, April 23, 1740). Thus he was started on his development of virtu—and he really did bring back a valuable collection of antiquities, particularly medals and pictures (to Middleton, April 9, 1743). Not long after his return home, he acquired in 1744 Conyers Middleton's collection, describing it as "a great antique purchase" (to Mann, June 18, 1744). Eventually, Strawberry Hill became noted for its virtu—it was a museum and art gallery as much as an original architectural achievement.

The tour gave Walpole the opportunity to develop his social sense, to converse with a variety of people. This conversational ease is unconsciously reflected in the grace and elegance that characterize his epistolary style. His knowledge of French and Italian enabled him to introduce foreign phrases into his writing with the ease of an accomplished linguist, thereby adding to the charm of his expression. It seems true to say that when he was on the tour he began writing letters seriously. A few written to West already exhibit an enviable style of liveliness and excitement, full of the speaking voice. Lastly, the tour gave him a feeling for some aspects of the Italian setting which he developed in *The Castle of Otranto* and *The Mysterious Mother;* and in this respect, too, the tour also confirmed his anti-Catholic prejudices.

At this time of his life, Walpole's religious beliefs were best developed in his second important literary composition and in his most ambitious effort in heroic couplets, "An Epistle From Florence to Thomas Ashton, Esq., Tutor to the Earl of Plimouth" (1740).[20] In this didactic verse (like his serious poem on King's College Chapel), Walpole asks that Ashton teach his pupil in the right spirit of the Ancients, inculcate "a love of freedom," and a "sane philosophy," and an admiration for the English Constitution in this young man who will enjoy the inestimable privilege of being British. He objects to "cloyster'd monkeries" and urges that Ashton use history to teach his student a generous liberal attitude toward life and society, and to develop in him a respect for liberty. He denounces kings and priests, and their unholy alliance; and he particularly objects to church support of the secular king's so-called divine right. He expresses disgust with the Royal Unction: "The Priest some blessed nothings mutters o'er,/Sucks in the sacred grease at ev'ry pore." Then he points to the papal dominions, evil and corrupt, where king and priest unite to oppress the people:

> Where fat Celibacy ursurps the soil,
> And sacred Sloth consumes the peasant's toil. . . .
> Oppression takes Religion's hallowed name,
> And Priestcraft knows to play the specious game.

His opposition to the priests—"Unlearned, unchaste, uncharitable Saints"—for their venality and hypocrisy, superstitious irrationalism and idolatry, sexual license, and even infant murders, sounds like militant Deism; and also it explains his hostility toward the villain priest in *The Mysterious Mother.* His opposition to "the Royal Will, that great prerogative of doing ill," is Whiggish, as is his linking the Roman Catholic Church to Jacobitism. The political implications of religion to a large extent may account for the venomously harsh tone of this poem. For example, he declares that gentle Charles I was corrupted by Rome, Charles II died a bigot, and William III chastised James II for "meditating to subvert the laws": "Thus have I try'd of Kings and Priest to sing,/And all the woes that from their vices spring."

Walpole never again wrote anything so powerful as this anti-Catholic invective; for his later verse, pretty and genteel, is of a complimentary and socially accommodating nature. However, he continued to express antipapist sentiment in verse, as in the epilogues to *Tamerlane* and to his tragedy, *The Mysterious Mother,* and in his characterization of

Father Benedict, the villain who is the instrument bringing about the catastrophe in his play. In prose, we find the gratuitously pejorative remarks about "an artful priest" in the Preface to the first edition of *The Castle of Otranto,* and numerous remarks scattered through his letters and journals. This theme appears so often in his writings as to suggest obsession, an interesting result of it being his profound distrust of Edmund Burke.

The militancy of the satire in the "Epistle to Ashton" suggests the depth of his political and religious commitment to the cause of Protestantism and the Hanovers. Walpole never relaxed from these politico-religious opinions. The Deism of the poem is also unmistakable, for it was influenced by Walpole's admired Conyers Middleton, the fiery Deistic controversialist, as Walpole himself admits (to Middleton, November 22, 1741). The same offenses that struck him provoked Middleton in *A Letter from Rome* (1729), a work "showing an exact conformity between Popery and Paganism," and proving that the "Religion of the present Romans was derived from that of their heathen ancestors." So Walpole, illustrating the incorporation of pagan beliefs into the Catholic Church, shows that "Prometheus' vulture Matthew's eagle proves," heathen loves become heavenly cherubs: Ganymede, an angel; Apollo, a saint; Jove, Saint Peter; and Astarte, Jewish Mary.

Walpole returned from the Continent to England in September, 1741, to become a member of Parliament for Callington, Cornwall, a pocket borough of his wealthy sister-in-law's family. He never visited Callington, yet represented it for thirteen years to 1754, when he was chosen for Castle Rising, Norfolk, which was under the control of his father's family. The early 1740's were a most difficult and painful time for the young man to enter politics, for the end of his father's long ministry was in sight. After twenty years of relatively tranquil rule, Sir Robert was facing downfall and defeat; and the son, still in his formative years, was tremendously affected (to Mann, October 19, 1741). Sir Robert was forced to resign on February 12, 1742, and was immediately raised to the peerage as earl of Orford with a pension of £4,000 a year. It was upon the motion of the Opposition to set up a secret committee to examine the conduct of Sir Robert's ministry for its last ten years that young Horace Walpole made his maiden speech, a defense of his father. This speech, a copy of which Walpole sent to Mann (March 24, 1742), appears to be somewhat cold; for we expect an impassioned defense. However, Walpole was young and inexperienced; and he certainly was not an orator. Perhaps, too, his reasonable tone was what the situation required. At any rate, the committee's investigation came to naught; and the earl of Orford, saved from impeachment, was permitted to retire from politics in peace.

This defense of his father, modest as it appeared to be, marked an important turning point in Walpole's life. It initiated him into politics, and, in a sense, into manhood, as it put him on a level of equality with his father. The immediate political effect, however, was a series of satires on the new ministry; the immediate personal effect was a close relationship with his father during the last three years of Sir Robert's life. When his father's paintings were removed in 1742 from his London house to Houghton, Walpole helped hang his picture gallery and was consulted in matters of art. The result of all this effort was the catalogue of his father's famous art collection in the *Aedes Walpolianae* (1743), a work that inevitably enhanced the quality of Sir Robert's virtu.

Horace attended his father throughout Sir Robert's last illness. After his father's death on March 18, 1745, in his sixty-ninth year, the twenty-eight-year-old Horace wrote to Mann, "All my interest and significance are buried in my father's grave" (March 29, 1745). But this is an expression of sentimental grief; for Horace kept on living and was now free to develop his own personality. In the years up to the time he leased Strawberry Hill in 1747, his social position was securely established: he was extremely sociable and had many friends who were men of wealth and good family, some involved in politics (Henry Fox, Richard Rigby), others interested in women and gambling (George Selwyn, Richard Edgcumbe, Charles Hanbury Williams). He himself enjoyed politics, women and gambling—as well as balls, masquerades, concerts, card and water parties, Ranelagh and Vauxhall parties, and the opera and the theater. He had his seat in the Commons, which could be almost permanent, if he wished. He had places for life, and his substantial income of £2,000 or more was assured (to Conway, July 20, 1744). Clearly, he did have a respectable reputation in his own right, for he was asked to supply an Epilogue to Nicholas Rowe's *Tamerlane,* which was produced on a special occasion at Covent Garden on November 4, 1746.

Walpole had been frightened by the Jacobite rebellion of 1745, which had just been suppressed. Had the Stuarts succeeded in returning, his fortune would most certainly have been lost. As son of the prime minister who had vigorously maintained the Hanoverian dynasty and implacably opposed the Stuarts, he might even have lost his life. Many letters about the Forty-five written to Mann and others make clear his agitation—and his relief after the defeat of the Pretender's son at Culloden in which, incidentally, Conway had distinguished himself by personal bravery.[21]

Although Walpole was a poet of fashion, he was thus the proper person to ask to perform this service, for in the Epilogue he could speak for himself as well as for all staunch Whigs. An angry poem, the Epilogue celebrates the victory over the Pretender's forces and affirms the political and religious principles which his father had done so much to establish. It may be described as an anti-Tory, anti-Jacobite, and anti-Catholic tract:

> Chains, real chains, our Heroes had in view,
> And scenes of mimic dungeons chang'd to true.
> An equal fate the Stage and Britain dreaded
> Had Rome's young missionary Spark succeeded.[22]

It is easy for Walpole who had recently seen the Pretender's family in Rome to make the connection between Catholic "bigotry" and Stuart despotism: "From foreign realms a bloody Chief is come,/Big with the work of Slav'ry and of Rome." He expressed with vehement anger his hostility to "monkish Laureats," censorious inquisitors, priests, and "blind zeal." Naturally, his feelings at the end of the rebellion spilled over into his letters. His accounts of the state trials which wound up the affair are among his epistolary masterpieces.[23]

As soon as the rebellion, the trials, and the executions were over, Walpole worked on his plan to establish a country retreat. He moved first to a small house within the precincts of Windsor Castle, near Gray's summer resort at Burnham Beeches, after the two had effected a reconciliation. Gray encouraged Walpole to write his memoirs; Walpole encouraged Gray to write poetry—and was eventually largely responsible for the publication of two of Gray's most famous poems, the "Eton College Ode" (1747) and the "Elegy" (1751). Dissatisfied with his place at Windsor, Walpole after a year leased another place just out of Twickenham (to Mann, June 5, 1747). With palatial Houghton Hall probably as his standard, he must have exaggerated the smallness of this ordinary square two-storied house with four windows on each side.

This modest structure which he enlarged by degrees became known as the famous Strawberry Hill; such was the "little plaything house" that he had bought from Mrs. Chenevix, the toy woman, and transformed into a toy castle, the inspiration of *The Castle of Otranto*. The improvement of this building occupied him practically the rest of his life. Strawberry Hill gave him the solitude he needed for all his other occupations—the writing of books and letters, his scholarship and the development of his connoisseurship, his collection of virtu.

In the mid-1750's, Walpole vividly described himself in a letter to Bentley as an alert but detached spectator: "In short, the true definition of me is that I am a dancing senator—not that I do dance, or do anything by being a senator; but I go to balls and to the House of Commons—to look on: and you will believe when I tell you that I really think the former the more serious occupation of the two: at least the performers are more in earnest" (March 6, 1755). We should not be deceived by the irony of this self-disparaging confession. It is a typical pose that Walpole affects in letters to some of his correspondents. True, his attitude appears to be supercilious, and he does communicate an impression of being a fastidious dilettante who could only dabble in politics, or in art. But he was really very deeply committed to these areas of activity, as his history and memoirs (which he had seriously begun in 1751 after some abortive attempts) and his literary and art criticism the *Catalogue of Royal and Noble Authors* (1758) and *Anecdotes of Painting* (1762–71), conclusively demonstrate.

In this period Walpole also contributed nine essays (1753–56) to *The World*, a periodical founded by Edward Moore, published by Dodsley, and designed for the world of fashion, unlike Samuel Johnson's *Rambler* and John Hawkesworth's *Adventurer*. In these essays, Walpole satirized lightly the return of nature, "real water," on the stage; William Kent's landscape gardening; the fauna and flora of the dessert table; the reformation of the calendar; the politeness of highwaymen (he himself was almost killed by one); the English, particularly elderly English "flames" or old women as objects of passion (ironically anticipating his relationship with Mme du Deffand); the barbarism of the Dark Ages; letter writing; the exiled Theodore, formerly king of Corsica; and his friend Henry Fox. Walpole wrote a more serious satire in his *Letter from Xo Ho* (1757), on the inconstancy of the English and their cruelty in executing Admiral Byng, whom he was unable to save, as he explains in his *Memoirs of George II*. This Chinese letter is now notable because the name of Xo Ho's correspondent, Lien Chi, was adopted by Goldsmith for his papers on the *Citizen of the World,* Lien Chi Altangi.

The publication of *Designs by Mr. R. Bentley for Six Poems by Mr. T. Gray* (1753), which Walpole encouraged, probably gave him the idea of setting up his own press, which he did four years later in July, 1757. He converted a little cottage on his grounds at Strawberry Hill into a printing office, staffed with never more than a man and a boy. The first important job was the printing of Gray's two Pindaric odes, "The Bard" and "The Progress of Poesy" (August, 1757). Soon came other important publications—Walpole's *Catalogue of Royal and Noble Authors* (April, 1758); *Fugitive Pieces* (Summer, 1758), which he dedicated to Conway; and *The Castle of Otranto* (1764). Altogether, Walpole printed thirty-four books, some of only a few pages, and seventy-eight "Detached Pieces"—title pages, labels for books, and cards of address. The number of copies ranged from two thousand of Gray's *Odes* to fifty of *The Mysterious Mother*, seven of *The Hieroglyphic Tales*, and a single title page. These press titles are now collector's items.

From the esthetic point of view, the most important period of Walpole's life is that between the purchase and reconstruction of Strawberry Hill beginning about 1750 and the composition of *The Mysterious Mother* and the meeting with Mme du Deffand about fifteen to twenty years later. He was at the height of his creative powers during these middle years; all his important imaginative works and all of his enduring critical works were composed between the ages of thirty-three and fifty-three. Thereafter occurred largely a refinement of his artistic ability in the form of letters, which did not require sustained effort. However, of course, the volume and quality of these letters suggest another and more generous interpretation—that there was no real slackening but a change in direction of his artistic powers.

Parliament was merely one of Walpole's many interests. By temperament he was unsuited to political leadership. In his own words to Mann on March 7, 1754, he was "a person who loves to write history better than act in it." His political journals on the reigns of George II and George III testify to the truth of his insight. Really, his political career was almost entirely devoted to furthering the military and civil interests of his cousin Conway. When Conway began in 1754 to take an active part in parliamentary debate, Walpole, working behind the scenes, began to advance his views through him, and in the next few years worked on behalf of Conway. At the outbreak of the Seven Years' War, Conway had to serve in the army again, resulting in Walpole's temporary inactivity. It was at this time, however, that he tried to save the life of Admiral Byng, but without success. Nor could he help his cousin, when General Conway was dismissed in 1757 from his post of Groom of the Bedchamber for displeasing the king by the failure of his expedition to Rochefort. Walpole could only express his sympathy in verses and letters (November, 1757).

Suffice it to say here that when Conway was once more dismissed in 1764 from the king's service for voting in Parliament against General

Warrants, Walpole, intensely furious, offered Conway his savings of £6,000 "in the funds" (April 21, 1764), and came to his defense with a pamphlet, *A Counter Address to the Public on the Late Dismission of a General Officer.*[24] In this polemic he attempted to prove that Conway did not deserve punishment for his conduct in Parliament. He declared that the "total" ruin of Conway, which the king intended, was cruel and barbarous—a type of action appropriate in France and Italy but certainly not in a free country. His most thoughtful argument was constitutional, an argument that underscored his Whig principles. Only Parliament checks and controls officers of the crown, he asserted, while the reverse is a subversion of the whole constitution as it has been established by the Revolution: "Does a member of parliament go out of his way who calls the highest officer of the crown to account? Parliament is the supreme court of this kingdom; nor has it been heard since the Revolution, that the meanest member in the house of commons is not authorized to question any minister, be he whom he will."[25] Walpole thereupon termed those who calumniated Conway to be Jacobites—they wished to extend the prerogative and destroy the unquestionable rights of Parliament. Undoubtedly, his anger and frustration, expressed in the summer of 1764 when he was working on, or had just completed, *The Castle of Otranto*, affected his fiction.

When, a year later (1765), Conway became leader of the House of Commons at the time of the Stamp Act crisis, he had an opportunity to reciprocate Walpole's goodwill. But he failed Walpole completely—he made him no offer of a place, nor did he attempt to protect a sinecure over which Walpole was tremendously concerned—a patent place that Walpole would lose upon his brother Edward's death. Naturally, Walpole was mortified by Conway's ingratitude, coldness, and neglect; and, in his disillusionment, he could no longer feel very close to this man whom he had idolized. But Walpole still had Conway's confidence; indeed, Conway frequently trusted him with secrets that he kept even from his wife and brother.

Walpole was certainly aware of Conway's failing and should have acted accordingly; but for some reason—was it pride?—he held back. It is surprising to see how often in the *Memoirs of George II* Walpole described Conway as "cold." True, he lavished praise on Conway in 1751 as a person with "a very superior understanding"—"one of the most agreeable and solid speakers in parliament." Recognizing his military ability and his bravery in battle, and citing the battles of Fontenoy and Laffelt in the 1740's and the raids on the French coast in the 1750's, Walpole described him as "cool and determined." In 1755 his oratory "soothed and persuaded," but he also "had a cold reserve, which seemed only to veil goodness." In 1760 he was a man of great integrity, in Walpole's opinion, with a "spotless virtue," characterized by "disinterestedness, and total alienation from all political intrigues." But an impartial estimate, which Walpole always tried to make in his memoirs, revealed one flaw which made real intimacy impossible: "Cold in his deportment, and with a dignity of soul that kept him too much above familiarity, he missed that affection from his brother officers, which his unsullied virtues and humanity deserved; for he wanted the extrinsic of merit." As for himself, Walpole frankly confessed his own "failings and blemishes," particularly that his "resentments were impetuous, and by no means of an accomodating [*sic*] mold."[26] Thus he gave the definite impression of being a vehement and passionate nature; but he must also have been a sentimentalist, for he craved a positive and visible sign of warmth and affection, which Conway, apparently much too self-centered, was unable to supply. Obviously aware of this failing in Conway, Walpole should never have allowed his cousin to hurt him. However, instead of provoking a quarrel over an affront which his friend was too blind to see, he ran off to France to escape a painful situation and, as he writes in his first *Paris Journal* (September 19, 1765), "to avoid politics," despite Conway's protests against his "desertion."

In Paris, Walpole sought another outlet for his feelings, and there soon found some consolation for Conway's failure in sensibility. His letters and *Paris Journal* indicate that he met, talked, or dined with hundreds of people in the best society and had scarcely time to rest.[27] He disliked the French opera (September 14, 1765) but enjoyed the *opéra comique* with its harlequin (September 22, 1765). At first, he found the Parisian *beau monde* dull, although he received a friendly welcome from the French whom he had entertained at Strawberry Hill. He disapproved of Rousseau and of the philosophes and *Encyclopédistes,* and of their outspoken skepticism and much too vigorous attacks on religious orthodoxy (to Montagu, September 22, 1765; to Gray, November 19, 1765). He saw them as atheistic subversives, destructive of religion and the monarchy (to Brand, October 19, 1765; to Conway, October 28, 1765). He noted that the reigning fashion favored Samuel Richardson for his sentimentalism and David Hume for his atheism and freethinking. (Hume was secretary to Francis Conway, Lord Hertford, the English ambassador.)

The ambassador, Conway's brother and Walpole's cousin, secured Walpole an invitation to visit Versailles. There, even in the palace,

Walpole, as he was being presented to the royal family, noted evidences of "parade and poverty" (to Lady Hervey and to Chute, October 3, 1765).[28] Walpole also bought a good deal of French china and did a lot of sightseeing; and, eventually, as he was invited to the famous salons of the aristocratic leaders of fashion, he met Mme Geoffrin and in October, 1765, "her great enemy" Mme du Deffand (to Gray, January 25, 1766), who was to become of great importance to him. In the fifteen years of their friendship, Walpole went to Paris for four more extended visits in order to see Mme du Deffand (1767, 1769, 1771, 1775); and they exchanged hundreds of letters until her death in 1780 at the age of eighty-four. The definition of their tragic-comic relationship is a fascinating psychological exercise. Yet, whatever the nature of their feeling for each other, to some extent it influenced Walpole's conception of his unusual tragedy *The Mysterious Mother*.

In 1765 when Walpole first met her, the Marquise du Deffand was about sixty-nine years old, in Walpole's words, "an old blind *débauchée* of wit" (to Conway, October 6, 1765). But it was not long before he looked upon her favorably and enjoyed her generosity and conversation (to Gray, January 25, 1766). He had met her through his friend George Selwyn, to whom he confessed that he supped at her salon twice a week, and that he bore "all her dull company for the sake of the Regent" (December 7, 1765). Apparently disturbed by radical infidel and republican thought, Walpole at this time of his life desired a taste of frivolous society, wit and gossip, not dangerous ideas. He found what he wanted in her circle—one in which, with the exception of the duchesse de Choiseul, whose husband was the leading minister, all the women were elderly and the men almost senile. But this decrepit and conservative salon attracted Walpole, now about fifty years old himself. He endured the others because he especially wanted to hear Mme du Deffand talk; and she had been the regent Orléans' mistress for two weeks, or so Walpole wrote to Gray (November 19, 1765). She was also familiar with some people who knew Mme de Sévigné (1626–96), a letter writer whom Walpole almost worshiped. Mme du Deffand soon became infatuated with him, although all he could feel for her was admiration, friendship, and a profound affection.

The origin of their relationship is found in their congeniality, despite their difference in age. They must have originally flattered their vanity by being in each other's company—she, the wittiest and most famous hostess in Europe; he, a son of the former prime minister and a close relative to the present British ambassador. It was a social triumph for both; but, even more, they shared conversation and wit, and they had just been betrayed by trusted friends—she, by her protégée Julie de Lespinasse (who broke with her the year before and stole the notable Turgot and D'Alembert and the *Encyclopédistes* away to her own salon); and he, by Conway. They were also lonely and out of harmony with the age. In outlook and attitude they were in general agreement— in their hatred of religious or political enthusiasm, for Mme de Deffand laughed at the clergy, miracles, and superstition, as well as at the *philosophes* (to Gray, January 25, 1766). The psychological moment for spiritual communion could not be improved; and it was inevitable that they soon developed a sympathy for each other that became in time, affection—or more, on her part.

From Walpole's point of view, their relationship endured because he saw in her the radiant and dissolute Regency court of the past. He loved the glamorous past, and she represented the world of the old regime in France, the world that was soon to vanish in the volcanic fires of the revolution. Furthermore, she was old—and posed no real threat to his emotions. She probably served as a mother surrogate, for that is the way (at least in the beginning) she occasionally saw herself with respect to him.[29] When she admired him, she restored his self-confidence; but, when she came to love him passionately as an old woman would, or could, he could not, or would not, reciprocate. He was constantly on his guard; he did not want to be hurt again, as he had been by Henry Conway. He confessed to his friend John Craufurd: "I am not at all of Mme du Deffand's opinion, that one might as well be dead as not love somebody. I think one had better be dead than love anybody" (March 6, 1766). Perhaps, also, on the deeper latent level, for him to respond overtly was impossible because doing so would have meant incest.[30]

In his verse "Portrait" (1766) of her, Walpole praises the marquise for wit, memory, fancy, judgment, reason, patience, and friendship which, to him, is the mean between sensual love and distancing and diffident pride.[31] He makes clear that their relationship must be based on friendship, not love. To say that he behaved cruelly and callously and that throughout their affair he was motivated by "an inexcusable egoism," as Lytton Strachey asserts, may be too severe.[32] But she herself in her prose portrait of him of November, 1766, noted that he lacked tenderness, and that his fear of appearing feeble made him act harsh; furthermore "vous êtes en garde contre toute sensibilité.[33] She also noted that he suppressed his feelings and checked his conduct for fear of being ridiculed, to her an unpardonable weakness, and that he had a horror of affectionate friendship caused by some great grief which he was unwilling to impart.

She certainly showed great insight in this character portrait; but she herself did not act in accordance with her penetrating reason. Her indiscreet romantic exuberance exasperated and embarrassed him, as it would any man under the circumstances. W. S. Lewis describes his reception of her extravagant passion as "nervous,"[34] but it may be more correct to say that his dread of ridicule was obsessive. And, also, perhaps he was not quite wrong to forbid her to use the word "love" in her letters to him. Their extensive correspondence, which continued for fourteen years until her death in September, 1780, was interrupted only by his visits to Paris in order to see her. Altogether, she had written over eight hundred letters to him. She bequeathed all her papers to him—he would not accept her money—and her little dog Tonton, which he faithfully cared for until its death.

In March, 1768, Walpole was about fifty-one years old. In February, 1768, he had published his *Historic Doubts on the Life and Reign of Richard III;* in March, he had completed *The Mysterious Mother;* and also in March, when Parliament dissolved, Walpole gave up his seat in the House of Commons. In the *Historic Doubts* he tried to prove that Richard was not guilty of the murders of Henry VI, the duke of Clarence, the two young princes, and his own queen, according to Thomas More's account; and that his physical deformity was grossly exaggerated. His argument was based on what he thought was the Coronation Roll of the king. But one of his antiquarian adversaries proved that this evidence was inadmissible, for it was merely a volume of Wardrobe Accounts not exclusively associated with Richard's coronation. After some controversy over this evidence, Walpole abandoned his theories. Walpole's work whitewashing Richard is significant as an expression of his antiquarian interests; and it may have been invested with some psychological meaning, too, as the discussion of *The Mysterious Mother* suggests.

Up to this time in 1768, Walpole was very productive; but after this time he accomplished nothing of substantial artistic or critical importance. When we consider the unity and structure of his life, it appears that Walpole disintegrated. True, he kept up his correspondence and his political journals, completed his *Anecdotes of Painting* (1771), and wrote an occasional crazy *Hieroglyphic Tale*—but that is about all. To Conway, he described himself as "always employed, and never busy; eager about trifles, and indifferent to everything serious" (August 18, 1774). Gray died in 1771; and a relationship that Walpole tried to establish with Gray's biographer William Mason did not inspire him to any great imaginative effort, although he did write many political letters to Mason and notes for Mason's satires. And in 1776 his close friend John Chute died, too, affecting him deeply (to Mann, May 27, 1776).

Nor did his occasional excursions to Paris or to English country houses and visits to art exhibitions excite him to be productive himself. Houghton, he knew, was being ruined by his nephew, the third earl of Orford: and there was nothing he could do to prevent the sale in 1779 of his father's collection of paintings to Catherine the Great of Russia, a transaction that broke his heart (to Mann, February 11, 1779, August 4, 1779; to Lady Ossory, February 1, 1779). The trouble with America also contributed to his general sense of frustration and depression, because he thought the administration's policy absolutely wrong and the Opposition which he supported, hopelessly weak and ineffectual. He appeared to have lost the zest for life, as he confessed to Conway (September 27, 1774): "What can I do? I see nothing, know nothing, do nothing. My castle is finished, I have nothing new to read, I am tired of writing, I have no new or old bit for my printer."[35] He seemed to retire to Strawberry Hill and to the amusements of the idle rich, the society of Twickenham whose petty old-maidish affairs he recorded in letters and verse. Only two episodes are biographically significant from this time to his death—those concerning Thomas Chatterton and the Berry sisters, Mary and Agnes.

The first attempt by the prodigy Chatterton to make the wealthy Walpole his patron was on March 28, 1769, when Walpole received from the boy of sixteen—a lawyer's apprentice—a short Ossianic poem on "Afflem," a glass painter; some verses on the death of Richard I written in the medieval style by "John seconde Abbate of Seyncte Austyns Mynstere the fyrst Englyshe Paynctere Yn Oyles"; and a discourse on "The Ryse of Peyncteynge Yn Englande, wroten bie T. Rowleie, 1469, for Mastre Canynge." In addition, Chatterton declared that he could help provide information about great painters of old Bristol for Walpole's *Anecdotes of Painting,* a second edition of which had been published in 1765.

Incredibly, Walpole, deceived by Chatterton's medieval imitations, desired further particulars. Chatterton thereupon sent more Rowley extracts on the history of painting and also tactlessly begged for help. This second letter made Walpole suspicious; and, when Gray and Mason declared the Rowley papers obvious "modern forgeries," Walpole tried to wriggle out of the relationship by means of a patronizing letter in which he gave young Chatterton prudent advice to stick to the legal profession. From this point on, he ignored the boy. But the superior and self-righteous tone of Walpole's letter angered Chatterton. In London, where Chatterton had gone in April, 1770, to try his hand at literature, Chatterton wrote some nasty satires against Walpole, whom he ridiculed as Baron Otranto in his *Memoirs of a Sad Dog* (1770); and, after four difficult months, unable to make any real headway in literature, the young poet killed himself on August 24, 1770, before he was eighteen years old. At the first annual banquet of Joshua Reynolds' Royal Academy, on April 23, 1771, Walpole was genuinely shocked to learn from Oliver Goldsmith of the young man's suicide. But it was not until 1778, when the editor of Chatterton's posthumous *Miscellanies* expressed indignation against "Baron Otranto, a distinguished literary character," for "treating Chatterton with neglect and contempt," and blamed him for the poet's untimely death, that the Chatterton-Walpole controversy began.[36]

The outcome of this tragic episode dimmed Walpole's reputation. Becoming the butt of sentimental journalism, he was accused of insensibility and ungenerosity; and, after the poet's death, the Chatterton legend converted Walpole into the heartless aristocratic murderer of youthful genius of the oppressed lower class. In the mythology, as developed by Anna Seward, for instance, Walpole appeared as "that fastidious and unfeeling being to whose insensibility we owe the extinction of the greatest poetic luminary, if one may judge by the brightness of its dawn, that ever rose in our or perhaps any other literature" (to Hardinge, November 21, 1787). Upon retrospect, however, it is dreadfully unfair to make Walpole responsible for Chatterton's failure in London and for his death from swallowing arsenic. Walpole had never seen or met Chatterton, never knew of his distress in London, nor was Chatterton indigent at the time of his correspondence with him.

Hurt and exasperated, Walpole tried to vindicate himself by explaining his conduct in a lengthy essay, two hundred copies of which were printed at Strawberry Hill (1779) for private distribution, and then reprinted with Walpole's permission and given wide circulation in four installments of *The Gentleman's Magazine* (1782) which the editor John Nichols described as a "satisfactory Narrative," an "elegant vindication of Mr. Walpole by his own very masterly pen."[37] After all, Walpole thought that he was being deceived and that Chatterton, or the person using him as a decoy, was laughing at him when he thought the Rowley forgeries were authentic. As Walpole wrote to Cole on June 19, 1777, "Macpherson's success with Ossian was more the ruin of Chatterton than I." Undoubtedly, had Walpole foreseen what did happen, he would have been warmly sympathetic and perhaps even generously philanthropic.

As Walpole grew older, his gout and rheumatism bothered him more; and, as his leisure grew, he spent more time at Strawberry Hill scribbling hundreds of letters, far more than ever before, and a good deal of time chatting and playing loo or faro with congenial old dowagers. His letters were the chief occupation of the last twenty years of his life; and at this time of his life they were like newspapers. His reviews of important public events lent weight to a correspondence ordinarily concerned, although vivaciously, with anecdotes of high society and entertaining trivialities—the latest bon mots, pregnancies, scandals. These epistolary comments on the American war, the Gordon riots, the trial of Warren Hastings, the speeches of Edmund Burke, and the debates between William Pitt and Charles James Fox complement his remarks in the political journals.

He enjoyed the company of women. John Pinkerton, who knew him well during the last ten years of his life, describes him as "an elegant and devout admirer of the fair sex, in whose presence he would exceed his usual powers of conversation; his spirits were animated as if by a cordial, and he would scatter his wit and petit mots with dazzling profusion."[38] As an old man, he was particularly attracted to young women, like Hannah More, the bluestocking whom he teased for her puritanism as his "holy Hannah," and the genteel young ladies Mary and Agnes Berry. These two women were only twenty-one and twenty-two years old when he met them for the first time in 1787; and he became very friendly with them a year later (to Lady Ossory, October 11, 1788). They were good looking, wellbred, charming, accomplished, witty, intellectual, and interested in him and his anecdotes of the past, which he wrote for them as his *Reminiscences of the Courts of George the First and Second* (1788).

He became very attached to them, especially Mary, just as old Mme du Deffand had been infatuated with him twenty years before. But he avoided ridicule and tried to obscure his feelings by simply exaggerating his affection, and by protesting his love for both women at once, calling them his "twin wives," his "dear Both," "my wife Rachel and my wife Leah," his "Amours." They proved to him that he had the capacity for deep feeling, and they restored his zest for life and for his occupations. They encouraged him not only to write the *Reminiscences* but to complete the *Catalogue of Strawberry Hill,* which he dedicated to them. When a cottage on his property at Strawberry Hill became vacant in 1791, he offered them the use of it because he wanted to have them accessible; and in his will he bequeathed it to them. The Berrys lived in this house close to Walpole for the remaining years of his life. Mary repaid her debt by providing an excellent edition of his *Works,* which was published one year after his death, although a large portion of the material had been prepared long before by Walpole himself.

Walpole's old age was made extremely happy by this relationship with the two women. But he almost went out of his mind with fears for their safety when they made a continental journey through revolutionary France from October, 1790, to November, 1791. At this time, London was becoming crowded with refugees, some of whom he had known in Paris. A few years later, he almost did lose Mary to someone else, but fortunately for him he never knew why. Mary, with the consent of her confidante, Walpole's favorite niece, Mrs. Damer (Conway's daughter), kept from him the secret of her love affair and engagement in 1795 with a General O'Hara. However, when the general had to return to his Gibraltar post, she refused to leave with him for fear of deserting the old and ailing man at Strawberry Hill, as well as her sister, who, also in the middle of a difficult love affair, was in need of her advice. Her engagement to O'Hara was soon broken, and they never met again. (Mary Berry lived for half a century more, to 1852, but never married; nor did Agnes, who lived quite as long.) Walpole was completely unaware of Mary's sacrifice.

When his nephew died in December, 1791, Walpole at seventy-four became the fourth earl of Orford. Houghton was now his. But the title and the property came too late to be really significant; the estate was encumbered with mortgages and, of course, lacked the art collection that had meant so much to him. At this time, therefore, Houghton brought only difficulties. He expressed his reactions in light verse, an epitaph which characteristically sums up his attitude toward life in the year 1792:

Epitaphium Vivi Auctoris

An estate and an earldom at seventy-four!
Had I sought them or wish'd them, 'twould add one fear more,
That of making a countess when almost four-score.
But Fortune, who scatters her gifts out of season,
Though unkind to my limbs, has still left me my reason;
And whether she lowers or lifts me, I'll try
In the plain simple style I have liv'd in, to die;
For ambition too humble, for meanness too high.[39]

We note that the first thought that came into his mind, after the expression of shock and surprise, was his fear of a wife and marriage—a seemingly gratuitous remark that unconsciously reveals one of the secret motives of his behavior, that his psyche feared erotic threats. Further, the declaration of the golden mean, really pretense for a man of his social standing and more than modest fortune, we may interpret as a defensive psychological maneuver by a Whig oligarch who had doubts about his life and secretly wished to do something significant and be thought important by his peers.

Walpole never took his seat in the House of Lords. In his last years, he simply dawdled away his time, writing letters or entertaining guests, for he was a celebrity noted for his Gothic castle at Strawberry Hill, his collection of virtu, his charming personality, and his witty conversation. In September, 1793, he did the honors of his home to the duchess of York and her suite; and one of his last important social events pictures this "quiet republican" elegantly entertaining in his castle another royal princess, Queen Charlotte, and eight other princesses. He worried about his gloves, and he wore a sword for the queen, he wrote in his very last letter to Conway (July 7, 1795), two days before his closest friend died.[40] We have an impression of a gallant old courtier, an image that brings to mind sentimental memories of the disappearing *ancien régime*. We can understand why the violence of the French Revolution appalled him. He felt like Burke; and, for the moment, his aristocratic conditioning and prejudices counted more than his radical Whig ideology. The destructive revolutionary violence showed how vulnerable he was; it was much too close for comfort. His friends among the French nobility were being destroyed; his past was being obliterated. Yet he also felt that the excesses of the revolution would retard the progress of civil liberty. To the end he remained faithful, in his way, to the libertarian principle. But he was an Old Whig.

When he was not entertaining at Strawberry Hill or playing cards, he spent his time conversing with his two "wives" or writing letters to Lady Ossory. His last letter to her—one of the very last of his enormous correspondence—is dated January 15, 1797.[41] He died six weeks later, on March 2, 1797, and was buried in the vault beneath the little church on the grounds of the Houghton estate.

CHAPTER 2

The Whig Politician

IN HIS *Description of Strawberry Hill,* Walpole noted a print that
hung in his own Bedchamber "of the house of commons and warrant
for beheading Charles I. inscribed with a pen, Major Charta."[1] In a
letter to George Montagu of October 14, 1756, he expressed the hope
that his correspondent would be "Whig enough to forgive" him for
decorating his bedroom with this curious but macabre document. Like
the notation in the *Description,* the letter is significant, for it explains
the intensity of Walpole's Whig attitude toward royal despots and the
importance of liberty: "on each side of my bed I have hung MAGNA
CHARTA, and the Warrant for King Charles's execution, on which I
have written MAJOR CHARTA as I believe, without the latter, the
former by this time would be of very little importance." Not long after
this letter, he began to compile *A Catalogue of Royal and Noble
Authors,* which was first published in 1758—a work that reflects his
uncompromising Whiggish, libertarian, and antimonarchical sentiments.
So far as our understanding of Walpole is concerned, this bibliography
is most significant not for its literary or esthetic content but for its
candid statement of a political principle which underlies his reading of
British history.

I *Defender of the Whig Faith:* A Catalogue of Royal and Noble Authors

Occasionally, it is true, Walpole does make a few critical comments
about literature in the *Catalogue.* For example, he expresses with his
usual severity a distaste for the "Romish clergy" and for popery, to
which he ascribed "the abolition of taste and literature"; but "the
revival of letters," he believed, "was one of the principal services
effected by the reformation" (*Works,* I, 279). He showed a good deal of
familiarity with the major and minor writers of the English Renais-

sance; and, in his opinion, the earls of Oxford and Dorset (Thomas Sackville) were probably responsible for the development of the drama (I, 332–33).

However, he has nothing to say of the possibility that Shakespeare's plays were written by the earl of Oxford, by Bacon, or any other noble author. He can neither fathom the reason for the immense reputation of Sir Philip Sidney, nor appreciate Sidney's experiments with the hexameter (I, 342, 345). He does not even so much as mention Sidney's sonnets. Nor does he care for Fulke Greville's experiments with the chorus "after the manner of the ancients; a pedantry as injudicious as Sir Philip's English hexameters" (I, 345). Ben Jonson's "pedantry" also was not worth imitating (I, 385); and Swift's *Four Last Years of the Queen,* "this wretched ignorant libel," could not help "falling into contempt and oblivion" (I, 430). Addison's opera *Rosamond* is "degraded below the buffoonery of Sadler's Wells by the stupid and false pleasantry in the personages of sir Trusty and Grideline" (I, 550 n. insert).

Coming to his own times, Walpole generously appraises the earl of Chesterfield's writings, even though Chesterfield was his father's enemy (I, 535–37, 545, 546, 550 insert). Finally, in one succinct paragraph he reviews the progress of English prose style from Dryden through Addison, Swift, Bolingbroke, and his mentor Conyers Middleton, in whom "our tongue . . . was raised to classic elegance and force" (I, 518–19). This is one of his most purely literary discussions in the *Catalogue.* It is a pity that Walpole did not see fit to develop his literary opinion in greater depth and with greater frequency. The critical remarks that are worth recording are casually made and relatively insignificant in comparison with his remarks on political history.

This work is important for two closely related reasons: personal, or psychological, and political. Psychologically, the *Catalogue* enabled Walpole to repay with a serious publication under his own signature his debt of gratitude to his father. In his first outburst of filial feeling included in this work, he expressed the hope that "to his father's virtues and merit may some impartial pen do as much justice" as he has done to one noble author, the admirable Edward Montagu, earl of Sandwich (I, 381), but, at this point, he writes no more. In the remarks preceding the catalogue of his father's works, he can only exclaim with feeling, "sixteen unfortunate and inglorious years since his removal have already written his elogium." But he weakly justifies the absence of an appraisal of the man's character and career: "it is not proper nor necessary for me to touch his character here" (I, 447).

In remarks added to later editions, he once notes with great satisfaction that, although his father "lost his power," he "lived to see justice done to his character" (I, 456). Lastly, toward the conclusion, he refutes at great length and with angry indignation a slander directed at his father's character and administration (I, 544–47). If these remarks mean anything, they suggest that, as Walpole became older, he became more sensitive to any tarnishing of the purity of his father's shining image. But such development of sentiment, if true, is not particularly remarkable; for Walpole had always admired his father, had always felt veneration for his memory. The depth and sincerity of his filial feelings may best be gauged by the intensity with which he maintained his father's Whiggish principles. He could not demonstrate his devotion to his father more genuinely or meaningfully than he did when he adopted and defended the Whig principle of liberty against the Tory one of the royal prerogative. This idea appears with such frequency in the *Catalogue* as to amount to an obsession.

The very nature of the subject, as indicated by the title *Royal and Noble Authors,* precludes an esthetic approach to literature. Because virtually all these authors were concerned with political affairs (possessing wealth and power, they inevitably became the leaders of the nation), Walpole perforce had to be concerned with politics. Time and again, as he writes about the Reformation, the Civil War, the Restoration, and the Glorious Revolution, he takes his stand against arbitrary power and Tories. To individual Whigs (first earl of Shaftesbury) or regicides (Cromwell) he may be occasionally hostile; but he always clings to Whig principles. The outstanding impression that this work makes on a present-day reader is simply that it is Walpole's Whig statement of faith.

Walpole does not go deep into the lives of the nobility. The character estimates, like those of the artists about whom he later wrote, are brief, occasionally pointed with wit, and superficially anecdoted; and the entries conclude with a list of literary productions. The method and approach are the same in the register of artists that make up the *Anecdotes of Painting.* He arranges the entries chronologically beginning with Richard I for the royalty and Sir John Oldcastle, Lord Cobham, for the nobility, and works up to his own times with his friends and enemies—Bolingbroke, the earl of Bath, John Lord Hervey, George Bubb Doddington, Richard Lord Edgcumbe, his father Sir Robert, and his uncle Horatio Lord Walpole. (Later additions include the earl of Chesterfield and Lord Clive.)

As he retails the lives of these authors, Walpole expresses his most cherished personal opinions on English history, his almost obsessive love of liberty. On the basis of his libertarian norm, which we may consider fundamental to his evaluation of history, past or present, Walpole thus criticized one of his idols, the chronicler of the Civil War, Edward Hyde, earl of Clarendon, stating that "the real sources of his fame" stem not "from his virtues" but "from his faults as a historian": Clarendon was inconsistent—"he acted for liberty, but wrote for prerogative" (I, 385, 388). Indeed, Walpole considered the central issue of English history—up to his father's attempt in his own time to stabilize the monarchy in the Hanoverian succession—as a struggle between the liberty of the subject and the royal prerogative. According to him, the object is to strike a proper balance between the two—such is his ideal of government. Clarendon, Walpole points out, had refused to support those who urged Charles II to be "absolute"; and, as a result of declining "to accept for him the slavery of his country," he lost the king's favor. Walpole then declares, in defense of Clarendon's policy, that he was "like justice itself" holding "the balance between the necessary power of the supreme magistrate and the interests of the people. This never-dying obligation his contemporaries were taught to overlook and to clamor against, till they removed the only man, who, if he could, would have corrected his master's evil government" (I, 386–87). To Walpole, the royal prerogative is extended only at the cost of freedom for the people, producing an evil imbalance. What is needed is to restore "the excellent balance of our constitution," which protects the subject as it did John Lord Somers and his own father (I, 432).

Walpole, who places the blame squarely on Charles I for upsetting this balance, believes that the king's execution was justified, for it followed from his provocation. The regicides, he asserts, more than once, "at worst but chastised the faults" of the monarch; "If a king deserves to be opposed by force of arms, he deserves death: if he reduces his subjects to that extremity, the blood spilt in the quarrel lies on him—the executing him afterwards is mere formality" (I, 393, 412; the latter page is mistakenly numbered 410).

Again and again, as he takes up one noble author after another, Walpole defends "those heroes who withstood the arbitrary proceedings of Charles and his ministers, and to whose spirit we owe so much of our liberty" (I, 357). He firmly maintains the Whiggish belief that the enormous exercise of the prerogative by the king and his ministers was the sole cause of the mischief: Charles I, he writes, "had found the crown in possession of greater power than is fit to be trusted in a single hand: he had exerted it to the utmost." The freedom of Parliament lies at the base of the people's freedom: Charles, Walpole continues,

wanted to humble, perhaps to enslave some free speakers in the house of commons, who possibly, by the bye, he knew were ambitious, interested, worthless men.—He did not know, or did not reflect, that by enslaving or silencing two or three hundred bad men, he would entail slavery on millions of poor honest men and on their posterity. He did not consider, that if he might send a member to the Tower, an hundred of his subaltern ministers would, without his knowledge, send a thousand poor men to jail. He did not know, that by his becoming king of the parliament, his lords, nay, his very custom-house officers, would become the tyrants of the rest of his subjects (I, 373).

It is tyranny, the usurpation of power by one man, that Walpole fears. Thus he questions if "Cromwell [was] a man to be tender of a constitution, which Charles the first had handled too roughly" (I, 380). Even the tyranny of the few he detests: the "aristocratic," he says parenthetically, "demonstrated by all experience to be the most tyrannous species of government, and never imbibed but by proud and self-interested men" (I, 393). Furthermore, as his argument according to the principle of constitutional liberty takes him in this direction, he comes to the radical conclusion (which he embeds in an angry footnote) that even the institution of monarchy may *not* be fundamental to liberty: "It is supposed that no country is so *naturally* propense to liberty as England.—Is it *naturally* propense to *monarchy* too?—Is monarchy the natural vehicle of liberty?" (I, 381 n; Walpole's italics).

Likewise, English imperialism in India proved distasteful to him because of its threat to liberty. In a harsh indictment of Lord Robert Clive, Walpole raged at "the invasions and depredations of his countrymen in India." He is ashamed of the applause received for "their devastations." But the danger to liberty from Lord Clive he fears most: "when heaven inflicts heroes on mankind, it generally accompanies them with their consequences, the loss of liberty—to the vanquished, certainly; to the victorious, often!" (I, 550). This echoes what he had previously written about George III's government's use of force to quell the American rebellion.

In view of his damning remarks on the monarch Charles I, the revolutionary leader Cromwell, and the imperialist Clive, we can describe his position with the much-abused present-day epithet "liberal." Thus, with this liberalism in mind, it is not surprising to see in the very last addition to the *Catalogue of Royal and Noble Authors* a harsh estimate of the French Revolution that matches Burke's emotional attack in the *Reflections,* a work that Walpole praised. The Terror aimed at the royalists, which he interpreted as the tyranny of the people, provoked Walpole's outburst of feeling: "since [1789] the follies of that nation have soured and plunged into the most execrable barbarity, immorality, injustice, usurpation, and tyranny; have rejected God himself and deified human monsters, and have dared to call this mass of unheard of crimes 'giving liberty to mankind'—by atheism and massacres" (I, 567). It is regrettable for the sake of complete consistency that Walpole succumbed to the hysteria of his class and thus failed to recognize any justice in the French "civil war." He did not join other liberals like Richard Price, Joseph Priestley, and Thomas Paine even in the early stages of the revolution in their support of the "Rights of Man," of liberty for all classes of people. He saw only the imbalance, the usurpation and the tyranny.[2]

But his ambivalence, if such it may be called, is only apparent. It is often pointed out by his biographers that, although he called himself "a quiet Republican,"[3] he prepared *A Catalogue of Royal and Noble Authors.* His republicanism, they say, is simply affectation. But the reasons for Walpole's "peerage" are not difficult to see—such as his compulsive antiquarian love of history, his national pride, his psychological need to identify with his father and, related to this last, his family pride. Chief among them was loyalty to his family. Certainly, he was proud to be able to range his father among the great peers who were the leaders of the nation and who, in his opinion, made its history; he was proud, also, to be able to note that his father was the last commoner to be honored with the garter (I, 381). Set among the nobility, Sir Robert shines forth as perfection itself, incapable of error. Apparently, when he made this register, Walpole did not believe anti-monarchist sentiments, opposition to arbitrary power and to the extension of the royal prerogative, to be inconsistent with homage to his father as one of the noble leaders of the people. As prime minister, Sir Robert had successfully demonstrated how the royal power could be so balanced by the Parliament which he led, as to produce stability and peace for twenty years. There is no doubt that Horace Walpole's quiet republicanism had clearly defined aristocratic roots. But, when times changed, when the French Revolution destroyed the monarchy as well as the aristocracy, republicanism was then tied to middle-class democracy, an association which Walpole's personal and upper-class sympathies made it impossible for him to tolerate. Thus his old Whig ideology of liberty, as in the case of Burke, was obviously inadequate for the changing times moving in the direction of social leveling. Walpole was consistent, but in terms of his own aristocratic liberal norm.

What he was soon to write after the *Catalogue* in the *Anecdotes of Painting* (1762) confirms this interpretation; for in it he made the following dramatic statement: "The cause of liberty was then [in the seventeenth century], and is always, the only cause that can excuse a civil war." The context for this declaration explains that he means *not* liberty for the people in general—on whom "the nobler motives" do not have "sufficient influence to save us from arbitrary power"—but liberty for his own class, on whom these motives are, of course, operable. He is severely critical of the base motives of the people upon whom "the slightest objects . . . make the deepest impression . . . . They seldom fight for a liberty of doing what they have a right to do, but because they are prohibited or enjoined some folly that they have or have not a mind to do" (*Works*, III, 197–98).

Another illustration taken from a time of social unrest makes clear his aristocratic position on liberty. The weavers, hit by a depression in 1765, wanted a bill for their relief passed by Parliament. When the bill was thrown out of the House of Lords by the duke of Bedford, the weavers rioted for many days, besieging the Parliament and attempting to destroy Bedford's London house. Thus, when the upper class was threatened by "the lower people," as Walpole calls them, he felt compelled to demonstrate his class solidarity, "lest it [his support of the relief bill] be construed" as sympathy with the weavers' cause: "I told the Duke, that, however I might happen to differ with him in politics, this was a common cause, and that everybody must feel equal indignation at it" (to the earl of Hertford, May 20, 1765). Walpole approved the use of military force in quelling the weavers' riots, which had, he thought, brought on a near "civil war" (to Mann, May 25, 1765). Such seems to be his attitude toward the French people rebelling against the *ancien régime:* a people's revolution is appalling to an aristocrat, even to a liberal aristocrat.

II   *The Theme of Liberty: The* Memoirs *and* Journals

Horace Walpole's intense commitment to politics is also seen in his extensive history of the latter half of the eighteenth century from 1751 to 1791 in the form of private memoirs and journals—*Memoirs of the Reign of King George the Second* for the years 1751–60 and first published in 1822; *Memoirs of the Reign of King George the Third* for the years 1760–72 and first published in 1845; *The Last Journals* for the years 1772–83 and first published in 1859; and the unpublished and fragmentary *Journal 1783–91*, which completes the series.[4] Although Walpole retired from the House of Commons in 1768, after twenty-seven years of membership, his political zeal did not diminish as these numerous and substantial volumes dealing largely with parliamentary affairs testify. The existence of these memoirs, on which he worked secretly for over thirty years, was revealed only to a few friends—Gray, Montagu, and Mme du Deffand.[5] Not meant for publication in his lifetime, these journals are a vast repository of important information about the politics of the period, about Walpole, about the ideas he cherished and about his most intimate relationship with his cousin Henry Conway, an important political figure.

From time to time in the *Memoirs of the Reign of George the Second,* Walpole explains his intention. At the beginning of the year 1754, for example, he declared that he did not intend to write a regular or formal history of his times. Wishing, however, to perform a service to historians who did, he simply threw together, as he said (I, 323),[6] some anecdotes and characters which shed light on the times in which he lived in order to give future historians an intimate knowledge of the men involved in policy-making: "I am no [solemn] historian: I write casual Memoires; I draw characters; I preserve anecdotes, which my superiors, the historians of Britain, may enchace into their weighty annals, or pass over at their pleasure" (I, 325). Unlike the plan of usual histories, he wrote in the year 1755, his is to avoid writing minutely of battles and sieges; it "is rather to develope characters, and the grounds of councils, and to illuminate other histories, than to compleat a history myself." He is basically concerned with policy-making in Parliament: "The decisions of actions and enterprizes shall suffice me" (I, 391).

Although he does not write a history in the old sense, one largely concerned with war, he does give some attention to military affairs, abstracting his information from newspapers and gazettes to supplement his private sources. Still, just as he said in the year 1760, he focuses on "civil annals. Whatever, therefore, leads to a knowledge of the characters of remarkable persons, of the manners of my age, and of its political intrigues, comes properly within my plan." This statement implies an emphasis upon "minutiae" and "small circumstances," facts generally overlooked by historians familiar to Walpole, including Voltaire (II, 410–11). As we would expect, his antiquarian zeal for detail lies behind much of the impulse to keep these journals; and he is satisfied, as he deals "minutely" with "court squabbles" and the like, to amuse his readers for a little while: "To be read for a few years is immortality enough for such a writer as me" (II, 227–28).

As part of fulfilling his intention, Walpole believes in telling the truth "rigidly" and impartially (I, 207–8). Such truth, to him, means facts, the virtues but also the stains and blemishes, irrespective of the politics of the English statesmen whose characters he writes (I, 208–9). For this reason, he knew, as he said to Henry Zouch on October 21, 1758, he could not write the life of his father. The truth, then, is the product of an attitude. The writer will be honest, and honesty is predicated upon the assumption of the fallibility of all mortals regardless of their position in society: "I shall not vary from the style I have assumed, but shall honestly continue to relate the blemishes of material personages as they enter upon the scene: and whoever knows the interior of affairs, must be sensible to how many more events the faults of statesmen give birth, than are produced by their good intentions" (I, 325). The last remark, a good example of Walpole's cynical wit, may explain why most of his portraits are so captious.

From our point of view, Walpole's conception of historical truth is not particularly complex. With regard to events (although he does not speculate on this particular aspect of the truth), his practice is adherence to facts, especially those generally unavailable except to the participating characters, and for which Walpole is at present the sole authority. Such truth refers to surface details about private conferences and conversations, secret intrigues and maneuvers concerning the formation of governments and the making of policy, as well as public speeches for which there are scarcely any records: who said what, when, where, and under what circumstances. With regard to characters, as he has insisted, the truth means a dispassionate acceptance of the impurity of human nature, of the baseness more than the virtue of man's motives. Any insight more complicated or more profound than this common-sense premise concerning the mixed motives of behavior is absent in the memoirs. We should not expect to see in his study of character any depth analysis that carefully explores the factors contributing to political action.

Incidentally, according to Walpole's own admission, the source-book value of the memoirs also suffers from other limitations. Besides generally avoiding the details of military strategy, Walpole deliberately neglects the facts of economics, candidly confessing his inability to comprehend this complicated subject (II, 327–28). Yet he does consider monetary greed an important motive, for he often mentions the distribution of lucrative sinecures, thereby demonstrating the truth of his aphorism, "Man is an aurivorous animal."[7] But government finances and problems of taxation (except from a purely political point of view) are never carefully detailed.

By and large, then, the *Memoirs* reflect the traditional concerns of the politically oriented historian—the affairs of royalty and the nobility and their roles as controlling agents, through Parliament, of government. But it must also be mentioned that Walpole does not so much as mention the many silent voters in this power structure—such as representatives of the small-landed interests—but prefers to focus on the outstanding figures. For the most part, these leaders whom he selected for his analytic portraits were the spokesmen of factions representing diverse political positions or prejudices. Because Walpole makes so much of it, oratorical eloquence must have been important to him. In sum, he was fascinated by the clash of personalities, to him the essence of politics; and so he thought of history as a drama performed by "the chief actors" (II, 333), whose highly personal affinities and antagonisms provided the motives for action.

A few themes are prominent. These appear frequently in other writings, but in the memoirs they are framed in an appropriate political setting and presented in greater detail. For example, as defender of the Whig faith, he had of course no use for the house of Stuart, which to him was characterized by "bigotry and obstinacy and want of judgment" (I, 251); and he vigorously condemns as absurd the three holidays dedicated to "a worthless and exploded race" (I, 369). He disliked Tory Oxford, "the sanctuary of disaffection" (I, 98). He had formerly recommended that "foolish" Charles I's relics "be given to that nursery of nonsense and bigotry, Oxford" (to Montagu, May 30, 1751). His memorandum (I, 263) on the education of the Prince of Wales (who was to become George III) also exhibits his hostility toward the arbitrary Stuarts and their supporters, the Tory Jacobites. This document expresses his alarm for Whig principles and the Protestant succession, and it touched off a stirring debate on the presence of Jacobites at court, a debate which resulted in a careful investigation of the future king's preceptors. As usual, Walpole's measure of a man's loyalty to the Protestant succession and the present British constitution is his attitude toward the Stuarts.

Likewise, Walpole is absolutely consistent in his attitude toward the royal prerogative, which, in his opinion, the Stuarts abused. A fear of exclusive power in princes of the blood, as we have noticed before, approaches obsession, and may therefore, along with the related policy of the exclusion of the Stuarts, be considered the master principle of his Whig politics (I, 349). In the record for 1754, he writes of his apprehensions for the constitution, sensing a growing threat of excessive power in the king: "from the ascendant which the nobility itself acquires each day in this country," among other causes, "prerogative and power have been exceedingly fortified of late within the circle of the palace." He then makes an important declaration of his political creed of liberty under a limited monarchy: "My reflections led me early towards, I cannot quite say republicanism, but to a most limited monarchy.... Republicans may prove objectionable as usurpers; yet republicanism as it tends to promote liberty, and patriotism as far as it tends to preserve or restore it, are still godlike principles.—" He calls himself a moderate, "a quiet republican," and expresses an attitude against violence and despotism to which he substantially adhered from youth to age, one consistent with his detestation of the atrocities of the French Revolution:

a republican who should be mad, should be execrable enough to endeavour to imbrue his country in blood merely to remove the name of a monarch, deserves to excite horror—a quiet republican, who does not dislike to see the shadow of monarchy, like Banquo's ghost, fill the empty chair of state, that the ambitious, the murderer, the tyrant, may not aspire to it; in short who approves the name of a King, when it excludes the essence; a man of such principles, I hope, may be a good man and an honest.... (I, 326–27)

Specifically, the source of his fears is found in the ability of the court party "to barter for power," that is, to purchase votes and thereby control the membership of Parliament and cause an extensive "breach of the constitution." He complained that "the auction of votes is become an established commerce" (I, 332–33).[8]

In a remarkable passage included in the same year (1754), he predicts the rebellion of the American colonies against the abuse of the king's prerogative. His attitude, as he describes how the duke of Newcastle exalted the dignity of the crown at the expense of the colonies, is exactly like that of the writers of the Declaration of Independence who placed the blame squarely on the king's usurpation of power: "the prerogative was strained unwarrantably over the [provincial] assemblies: the instructions to Sir Danvers Osborn, a new governor of New York, seemed better calculated for the latitude of Mexico and for a Spanish tribunal, than for a free rich British settlement, and in such opulence and of such haughtiness, that suspicions had long been conceived of their meditating to throw off their dependence on their mother country" (I, 344). Such being his attitude, it is no wonder that he objected to the court party's arbitrary and ruinous American policies during the first two decades of the next king's reign.

Obviously, this uncompromising Whig insistence on liberty is at the core of Walpole's political personality. This is one idea he shared with his father, who, as the son describes him, "never gave up his party to serve himself" (I, 200) and who kept Lord Bolingbroke and the Tory Jacobites in check. He recognized his father's limitations, but concluded that, although Sir Robert was not particularly intellectual, "he knew mankind ... consulted their interests ... intended their happiness": "he meant to serve mankind, though he knew how little they deserved it—and this principle is at once the most meritorious in one's-self and to the world" (II, 272–74).

This intense Whiggism also accounts for his factiousness, and, paradoxically, for his liberalism and humanity; while, at the same time, it explains a good deal of his behavior including his enduring attachment to his father and to his cousin Henry Conway. As a matter of principle, he suspected the worst of people in power; therefore, he enjoyed playing the role of parliamentary watchdog:

Every topic is treated in parliament as if the liberty and fate of the country depended on it: and even this solemnity, often vented on trifles, has its use. The certainty of discussion keeps administration in awe, and preserves awake the attention of the representatives of the people. Ministers are, and should be, suspected as public enemies: the injustice arising to them, or the prejudice to the country of such jealousy, can hardly ever be adequate to the mischief they may do in a moment, if too much is left to their power, if too much trust is reposed in their integrity. (II, 6)

Thus, because he trusted scarcely anyone with power, he "always leaned most to a man in opposition" (II, 18) and possessed an "ardour for factious intrigues" (II, 91). The importance of this idea can be gauged by the fact the he considers it first in his candid estimate of his own character (written 1758), and couples it with his father and his early conditioning: "Horace Walpole, without the least tincture of ambition, had a propensity to faction, and looked on the mischief of civil disturbances as a lively amusement. Indignation at the persecution raised against his father, and prejudices contracted by himself, conspired with his natural impetuosity of temper to nourish this passion" (II, 334).

His factionalism, which derived from his sympathy with the opposition or the underdog minority, always had the purpose of protecting the liberty of the individual subject from the infringements of superior arbitrary power. Thus he thought the treatment of Admiral Byng, court-martialed and sentenced to be executed for the loss of Minorca to the French, vicious and unjust; Byng was merely a convenient scapegoat for an inept administration (II, 119–20). Walpole inspired a parliamentary inquiry into all the circumstances involving this grisly affair, even though he personally disliked the man, but failed to prevent Byng's execution. Evidence of his compassion and humanity can be seen in his sense of guilt at having merely prolonged the victim's torment for two weeks during which the unsuccessful debate and investigation were in progress (II, 191–192). He also opposed the Marriage Act (which prohibited children from legal marriage without the consent of their parents) as an unjust and inhumane law. He thought that it undermined individual liberty and, as it protected families with large fortunes, encouraged pride and aristocracy, "that bane of society, that golden grate that separates the nobility from the plebeians" (I, 299, 311; II, 6).[9]

Further, he supported an act that permitted the naturalization of the Jews, which "superstitious bigots" in the Commons repealed under the influence of a fanatical mob, thus demonstrating "how much the age, enlightened as it is called, was still enslaved to the grossest and most vulgar prejudices" (I, 310). Moreover, he voted against the rigorous clauses in the Mutiny Bill (I, xlii). Lastly, and what is by far most significant, he supported the bill for the extension of the habeas corpus, "the cornerstone of our liberty" (II, 286). This bill, the object of which was to give support to the civil authority against arbitrary judges appointed by the Crown, was passed almost unanimously by the House of Commons. It was understandable to Walpole why the king opposed the bill, for it conflicted with prerogative (II, 295); but he was extremely bitter at the peers in the House of Lords for opposing it and preventing its passage in 1758.

To Walpole, as to us in the enlightened tradition of Western European civilization, the human right to freedom is natural and inalienable—in his words, an "immutable right" (II, 297)—and it cannot be authenticated by history or precedent: "Can ages of ancestors submitting to tyranny impeach my freedom? Have I not a right to be free, the moment I have the power of being so?" (II, 288). This right is at the heart of his interpretation of what happened in English history when the Stuart James II was deposed and later, at the death of Queen Anne without heirs, when the house of Hanover was established by Parliament over the house of Stuart: "The constitution, as settled at present, is in a king elected by the voice of the people without any right of succession, in opposition to an arbitrary family, and tied down from acts of violence against the liberty of individuals by that peculiar fundamental law, the act of Habeas Corpus" (II, 294–95). This declaration of principle underlies his passionate support of Conway who, when he voted against the legality of General Warrants in the next decade, was fired from his two positions under the Crown, thereby being deprived of his profession and losing practically all of his income.

It is because of its revelation of the author's character, the man as politician, that the *Memoirs of George II* is most interesting to us today. Although Walpole was correct in assuming that historians would find his facts and anecdotes curious and informative, we are attracted to the work because we see in it the image of a humane individualist vehemently attached to the spirit of liberty and nonconformity—with a redeeming and softening dash of good humor to suggest warmth and flexibility. And so, he concludes his frank and congenial estimate of himself: "In short, such was his promptness to dislike superiors, such his humanity to inferiors that . . . he thinks . . . had either extreme of fortune been his lot, he should have made a good prince, but not a very honest slave" (II, 337).

In the sequel to the journal of the last ten years of the reign of George II, *Memoirs of the Reign of George the Third,* Walpole discusses domestic and foreign events from the accession of the new king in 1760 to the beginning of 1772. In 1768, however, he quit his seat in Parliament; "consequently," he admitted, "what traces of debates shall appear hereafter must be mutilated and imperfect, as being received by hearsay from others, or taken from notes communicated to me." His "information was often incomplete," and "the mysterious springs of several events" eluded him. But he maintained his contacts with the leading politicians who were his sources: and he continued his narrative because, as he confessed, "it amuses me. I like to give my opinion on what I have seen" (III, 124).[10] Then he rationalizes his pleasure by underlining his moral purpose: "I wish to warn posterity (however vain such zeal) against the folly and corruption and profligacy of the times I have lived in" (III, 125). The most significant of these evils constitute the major themes.

Walpole chose 1771 as the terminal date of the memoirs because to him it was the climax of a period. At that time the country was at peace. What was to come, he intimated with bleak pessimism, was the destruction of the empire—the result of the king's illegal and vicious assertion of his power. Such is the major theme developed in these memoirs, a Whig interpretation of history. This view taken by Walpole—also by Edmund Burke—has generally been adopted by historians to explain the direction of events in the reign of King George III. Only in the last few years has it been challenged by Lewis P. Namier and his associates.[11]

In the course of his narrative, Walpole inserts his usual essays, most of them severely caustic, on the characters of the chief persons: the young King George III, George Grenville, Colonel Barré, the marquis of Rockingham, his cousin and close friend Henry Conway, Charles Townshend, Edmund Burke (and he also contrasts the oratorical powers of Burke and Townshend), John Wilkes and his henchman the poet Charles Churchill, the duke of Grafton, Lord North, the duc de Choiseul (the chief minister in the court of Louis XV), William Beckford (the lord mayor of London and the father of the writer). There is also much on the decline of Pitt, who in 1766 was advanced to the peerage to become the earl of Chatham at the cost of public esteem (II, 254). The brief sketch of Samuel Johnson suggests the nature of the "impartial" tone adopted in some of the characters:

With a lumber of learning and some strong parts, Johnson was an odious and mean character. By principles a Jacobite, arrogant, self-sufficient, and over-bearing by nature, ungrateful through pride and of *feminine bigotry,* he had prostituted his pen to party even in a dictionary, and had afterwards, for a pension, contradicted his own definitions. His manners were sordid, supercilious, and brutal, his style ridiculously bombastic and vicious; and, in one word, with all the pedantry he had all the gigantic littleness of a country schoolmaster. (IV, 196–97)[12]

But as Walpole said in self-defense, "I have spoken of every party and faction favorably or unfavorably as I thought they deserved . . . and that is all I mean by calling myself impartial" (IV, 85). Apparently, he was more concerned with giving his sincere opinion than in trying to be objective in his judgment. When he spoke of being impartial, he probably meant that he avoided flattery and abstained from being *partial* to anyone.

As in the preceding memoirs, where he presents a critique of the oratory of the period, Walpole includes an essay on the literature of the years 1760–67, a period which, he points out, was dominated by politics (III, 117–23). Thus he compliments Burke and notes the crude force of "the gross and virulent libels of Wilkes": Wilkes "first dared to print the most respected names at full length," setting a precedent for the daily and evening newspapers. He merely mentions Goldsmith "who meddled not with politics," but elaborately praises minor figures like Christopher Anstey (*New Bath Guide*), Hugh Dalrymple (*Rodondo*), and Richard Bentley (*Patriotism: A Mock Heroic*).

Tyranny, the major theme of these memoirs, appears in the minor episodes, such as the riot of weavers, as well as in the major occurrences of the decade: the Wilkes affair and the American Stamp Act crisis.

Walpole announces his basic interpretation of events in the introduction to the very first section. The source of the danger to the balance and stability of the country in George III's reign, despite auspicious beginnings, was the state of affairs at the court: the relationship between the king's mother, the Princess Dowager, and her paramour Lord Bute, the king's "Favourite." "A passionate domineering woman, and a Favourite, without talents, soon drew a cloud over this shining prospect" (I, 4). These two exerted a compelling influence on the young king, who was taught "cool dissimulation" by his mother and who was "under the influence" of a "haughty" aristocrat (I, 5, 28). The war against France was pushed half-heartedly; but, even when successful, the peace concluding it was "shameful" (I, 5), the cause for the bad peace found in the machinations of "the private Junto" (I, 8). For "it was sedulously whispered by the creatures of the Favourite and the mother that the plan was to retain all the late King's ministers, but that his Majesty would not be governed by them, as his grandfather George II had been" (I, 8). This policy, because opposition was divided, "soon carried everything in favour of Prerogative . . . and brought the country to the brink of ruin" (I, 9).

Soon Walpole saw Jacobites and Tories returning to court and insinuating themselves into entrenched positions everywhere under the protection of the Scotch "Favourite" (I, 12–3). "They abjured their ancient masters [the Stuarts], but retained their principles. . . . Prerogative became a fashionable word" (I, 13). Moreover, the court "conducted themselves by the advice bequeathed by Lord Bolingbroke [Sir Robert's chief Tory antagonist] who had, and with truth, assured the late Prince of Wales [the king's father] that the Tories would be the heartiest in the support of prerogative" (I, 42). Walpole says that he was prepared to accept a new administration under the new king, "had not the standard of Prerogative been hoisted, and disgrace [by the peace] brought on this triumphant country" (I, 167). The court was able to purchase a majority of votes to approve the peace, even though it was obviously a poor one (I, 157).

We can imagine his anger and concern when he learned that the majority in Parliament voted, in 1763, to observe a Jacobite Fast Day honoring the martyred Charles (I, 190). Alarmed by these reactionary evidences of a trend to the Stuart past, Walpole suspected only the worst of the new monarch: "no doubt can be entertained but a plan had been early formed of carrying the prerogative to very unusual heights" (I, 14). Encouraged by the court's partiality, "the Tories displayed their old prejudices and resentments" against the Whigs, "who in power, property, and credit were beyond comparison the preponderating part of the nation" (I, 109).

Walpole saw many signs of the court's assertion of power. In 1761 the king used his own revenue to corrupt electors and candidates in order to assure a properly disposed Commons (I, 31). Walpole himself, indirectly through his nephew Lord Orford, was frankly offered a bribe in order to secure his vote. But Walpole refused to influence his nephew or to support the administration, with the result that, in 1762, when payments from his own sinecure place were stopped "for some months," he suffered no little hardship (I, 167–72). Also, the chief minister, Henry Fox, formerly his close friend, failing to bribe him, granted the reversion of a place he shared with his brother Edward to "young Martin."[13] A few years later, Walpole noted that even the parliamentary persecution of Wilkes was owing to the king's possessing the resources to buy votes (III, 220).

This corruption Walpole had taken for granted when practiced by the Whigs under his father; but, when it was adopted by the court, he feared an imbalance in government. For, according to his old-fashioned Whig views, the safety and stability of the state depended upon maintaining a proper balance of the three parts of the constitution— king, lords, and commons. This meant that the best government is mixed, or a limited monarchy. In his critique of Mrs. Macaulay's doctrines, he rejected a republican form of government because it provides no check upon the people and the best citizens fall "a sacrifice to the ambition and envy of the worst" (I, 122–23).

A corollary of this basic principle of constitutional government as a balance of three forces guaranteeing liberty is the need for political parties. This, too, of course, relates to Walpole's belief, stated in the preceding *Memoirs,* that factionalism is essential as a preventative of arbitrary government. Political parties, he declared, were "the preservative of a free government." But when the king "succeeded . . . in breaking all parties, what was the consequence? that everybody ran to court, and voted for whatever the Court desired" (II, 270). With a majority of the Commons bought and with the Peers Tory in their bias, it was no wonder that in his time Walpole feared the worst for liberty in Great Britain. From the point of view of the present, however, it is interesting to see how modern and democratic Walpole's political principles are. Certainly, these so-called Whig principles account to a great extent for the enduring stability of the system of checks and balances that structures the American democratic republic.

The Wilkes affair provided additional evidence to confirm Walpole's thesis. John Wilkes, a member of the Commons, denounced the treaty of peace and insulted the king in the forty-fifth number of his publication, *The North Briton* (April 23, 1763). As a result of alleged sedition, he was seized on a General Warrant. The issues were the legality of such indefinite warrants (which resembled the much abused French *lettres de cachet*) and the immunity of a member of Parliament from arrest for exercising his privilege, his freedom of speech. Walpole follows the lengthy debates in Parliament, all the proceedings against Wilkes, which eventually resulted in Wilkes being declared an outlaw after he escaped to France in 1764 and then, upon his return a few years later, his three unsuccessful attempts at taking the seat in the Commons to which he was elected. Although Walpole personally detested the man, he "wished well to Wilkes' cause against prerogative" (III, 139) and opposed all the arbitrary proceedings against him. Because the Crown always aims at power, Walpole assumed, it tries to annihilate the liberty of the press by misrepresenting liberty as libel or license; and, when the Crown precludes members of Parliament from printing their grievances, then the liberty of all other persons is endangered. Thus the House of Commons in its arbitrary dealings with Wilkes "sacrificed him and their own privileges" and, following Walpole's argument, failed to act its role as the proper check on the king's power (I, 255-57). From Walpole's point of view, the evidence was unmistakable that it was a corrupt House that accepted General Warrants, the same that voted the faulty peace.

Later, in 1768–69, when Wilkes returned from exile and was elected three times to Parliament by the Middlesex electors and each time expelled by the obsequious majority, Walpole again blamed the court, King George, the Princess Dowager, and Bute for the persistent persecution of Wilkes (III, 199). Walpole and his friend Conway opposed the expulsion for the usual reason. The majority party could purge the House of all that are disagreeable to them, and "the danger to the Constitution is augmented when it is notorious that the majority is, of late years, almost always sold to the Court. There would be an end to Opposition, and consequently of liberty, if the Crown might garble the House of Commons at will" (III,173).

Walpole was involved in the Wilkes-and-liberty crisis not only ideologically but also personally. How intense was his commitment to Whig political principles may be seen in the following episode which he narrates with great passion. Two general officers, including Walpole's closest friend General Conway, were dismissed from their regiments because they voted against General Warrants and for the privilege of Parliament. (Conway was dismissed at the end of the parliamentary session in April, 1764.) To Conway, this loss of position was very serious, because it meant the loss of a substantial portion of his income as well as the loss of his profession. When Walpole learned of these dismissals, he angrily denounced them as tyrannical. He was told that "the King could not trust his army in such hands." His reaction to this message from William Pitt is vivid; we can visualize his great tension: "I started! 'Good God!' said I, 'Mr. Pitt, what are they going to do with the army? to what use is it to be put, if a man of Mr. Conway's virtue, and tried loyalty and bravery, cannot be trusted with a regiment! You alarm me!' He beat about backwards and forwards; sometimes it was offers and promises, sometimes threats; but I had taken my part, and had got hold of words I was determined not to part with or forget" (I, 271). But not only was Conway dismissed from the command of his regiment of dragoons, he was also "turned out of the King's bedchamber" (I, 320). Walpole was stunned by this punitive retaliation against an officer for a single conscientious difference of opinion with the administration, to him a step "almost unprecedented" (I, 321). For it meant that "military men in Parliament were to forfeit their profession and the merit of their services, unless implicitly devoted to the Court" (I, 321–22).

Disgusted by the inability of the pathetically disorganized and supine opposition to take advantage of the court party's temporary weakness in the face of the strong sentiment against General Warrants and tyranny, Walpole determined to give up politics (I, 319). For Conway, abandoned by his own family and without any friends (Conway did not immediately join the Rockingham forces), inspired his sympathy and support; and so, because he felt guilty at having advised him at such tremendous cost, Walpole generously offered Conway £6,000 and altered his will, giving him almost his whole fortune unless Conway's regiment should be restored to him (to Conway, April 21, 1764). Then, under shock, Walpole retreated to Strawberry Hill where, as he says, "I shut myself . . . for three days, till I had conquered the first ebullitions of my rage" (I, 325). Despite the intensity of his wish to quit politics, he returned to London and tried to help by means of a publication—*A Counter Address to the Public on the Late Dismission of a General Officer.* This pamphlet went into four editions, and Walpole himself thought it a success (II, 7). But clearly it was not enough to help his friends in the opposition who, he thought, were timid, cautious, lacking fire. They slept, but Walpole spent many sleepless nights worrying over his helplessness. At one point, payments on his own position were also stopped. He was made so desperate by his frustrations in the spring and summer of 1764 that he thought he had only enemies. He even talked of the possibility of civil war! Then frightened by his temerity, Walpole drew back at the idea of violence: "My nature shuddered at the thought of blood, and I felt what every good man will feel in civil commotions, *that there is nothing so difficult as to make the people go far enough, and prevent their going too far"* (II, 2; Walpole's italics).

All through the summer of 1764, Walpole writes, he tried to form an active opposition (II, 21—22). But Conway, cold to the idea, rebuffed and thereby mortified him (II, 22—23). Pitt refused to lead; Rockingham was, as usual, silent. The members of the opposition, disunified, leaderless, lifeless, and too few in numbers, were helpless. At this point, Walpole in disgust and despair at the futility of it all reiterated his determination to quit Parliament, "that splendid theatre of pitiful passions; not from having been too good for my company, but ashamed of being one of such Dramatis Personae" (II, 7). However, despite all this agonizing soul-searching, Walpole did not immediately quit; and an opportunity soon came for his friends to take control of the government. But the new ministry produced even more disappointment for him and undoubtedly cured him for good of active politics.

Grenville, in order to make the Americans help maintain their own army, planned in March, 1764, to raise revenue in the colonies. The measure—the notorious Stamp Act—passed through Parliament quietly, without any substantial opposition. The violent American reaction came as a surprise to the English. Writing in 1768, a few years after the events in early 1765—after the riots and protesting petitions from mutinous Americans and from native merchants who held American debts and who were dependent on colonial trade, and after the usual wrangling debates in Parliament—Walpole recognized the threat to good relations between the mother country and its colonies. In disgust, he called the act to tax the colonies a "fatal plan" (I, 309) that "set both countries at variance . . . threatening a scene of long and terrible calamity both to England and her colonies!" (I, 310) He foresaw, now that the colonies had become so opulent and powerful, "how difficult it would become for so small an empire as Britain to contain them within the necessary limits of dependence" (II, 49), and how precarious England's hegemony over them would be, placing "a greater military force in the hands of the Crown than would be consistent with the freedom of this constitution" (II, 49–50).

Walpole outlined the dispute between the two countries and, writing in January, 1769, stated his position, which resembled that held by Lord Rockingham and Edmund Burke in its caution and moderation: "Both policy and humanity, in this great contest between Britain and her colonies, should rather use their efforts to reconcile their interests than to pronounce between them" (II, 54). However, he went beyond Burke by asking that colonial subjects be treated equally with those of Britain: "Equal claim to indulgence and lenity of treatment with other British subjects should be ascertained to the colonies, if under the same jurisdiction" (II, 54). He is aware of the difficulty of attempting to compromise differences; and he is not exactly sure of the best solutions to the problems of colonial taxation and representation in Parliament and so can only urge "moderate counsels" on these nice questions (II, 55). "It is the kindest way of ruling men to govern them as they will be governed, not as they ought to be governed" (II, 55). If such wisdom had guided the obstinate majority—George Grenville and the stern and relentless defenders of the rights of Great Britain over the colonies— there might not have been an American War of Independence.

Meanwhile, the summer of 1765, after the king's differences with the ministers over the Regency Bill, brought in a new administration under Rockingham. Conway became Secretary at War; and, when the time to vote came, he supported the Rockingham ministry's "virtuous, honest, prudent, humane, and brave" (II, 156) decision to repeal the Stamp Act. It was brave because the spirit of surrender and weakness implicit in the repeal would certainly suggest treason. Therefore, to assure passage of the bill to repeal and a proper patriotic attitude, the ministry also argued that a Declaratory Bill of Right be passed—one that asserted as a matter of fundamental principle Parliament's right to tax the colonies. Throughout the crisis, Walpole was often consulted by the leading figures. Indeed, he was very actively engaged in the exciting politics of this whole period in the years before and after 1765.

Again, as in the affair of Wilkes and General Warrants, Walpole was personally as well as ideologically engaged; and again his story involved Conway (II, 149–52). Not long before, as he says, he "had entered into opposition on the view of the violent measures, and still more violent designs of the Court," and in so doing, to demonstrate his disinterested attachment to principle, he had truly "risked an easy ample fortune" (II, 149). It was therefore natural for him to think that, were his party successful, he "should obtain to have the payments of his place settle on some foundation that should not expose [him] to the caprice or wanton tyranny of every succeeding Minister. . . . My wish of making this independence perfectly easy, I had hinted to Mr. Conway during our opposition. He received it with silence. It was not in my nature to repeat such a hint" (II, 149).

In July, 1765, when the Rockingham ministry was formed, Conway, now redeemed, had a position of power in the new administration and was able to protect himself and his friends. Walpole expected an offer "of some considerable employment, which my vanity would have been gratified in refusing." When Conway informed him of the proposed arrangement of places, however, he was mortified to learn that his name was not even mentioned. His pride was so badly injured by this neglect that it was all Walpole could do to prevent dropping "a word of reproach on a friendship so frozen" (II, 150).[14] Yet he succeeded in keeping control of himself, and he still made the most of his close relationship with his friend even though Conway "had none of the warmth of friendship" (II, 151).

Then Walpole resolved to leave for France for a holiday, despite Conway's objections to the desertion, because "His insensibility had made me insensible" (II, 152). Although he could not beg for a favor himself, he desired before he left that his good friend Sir Horace Mann, the British resident at Florence, be raised to the rank of ambassador, which was immediately done. Undoubtedly, this whole affair, as it undermined Walpole's ego, contributed to his general pessimism and bitterness over the direction of events at home and his sense of overwhelming weariness which were expressed in his oft-reiterated wish to resign from active participation in politics.

After the repeal of the Stamp Act, a new ministry under Charles Townshend, eager to compel the Americans to submit to English authority, urged a policy of additional taxes on the colonies, a policy "of force and punishment," thereby opening up "the wounds scarce skimmed over by the repeal of the Stamp Act" (III, 24n.). Walpole also asserts in the same note, representing a revision of his original thoughts, that taxes were "instigated by the secret cabal at Court": "thus the ambition of the Court began the quarrel; . . . and the Crown, that delighted in the mischief, ended with being the great sufferer, and America happily became perfectly free" (III, 24n.). To Walpole, then, liberty—at home and abroad—against any possibility of tyranny was the real issue. His Whiggism is absolutely consistent, and Whig liberty is his measure of history.

Because it is important to an understanding of his interpretation of the forces that made history in this period, we must note that Walpole thought there was ample evidence of Lord Bute's secret machinations, despite the "Favourite's" protestations to the contrary. To Walpole, Bute "was really Minister still; and . . . no favour could be obtained but by paying court to him" (II, 206). Walpole blames the chaos he saw at home on the conduct of the king who encouraged Bute to lead a secret cabinet. With respect to America, the advice emanating from this second cabinet eventually led to the dissolution of the empire because, to maintain his power over the king, Bute tried "to prevent the diminution of the Crown's authority, by relaxation towards the Americans" (II, 208). Besides, Lord North, whose administration was responsible for managing the country during the crucial decade of the 1770's, "was no more than the passive instrument of the black designs of the Court." North "had flung himself into the hands of Lord Bute's junto" (IV, 56, 61). During North's administration, "the court found all their facilities for governing by corruption and influence return. Every question was carried in both Houses by more than sufficient majorities" (IV, 57).

Walpole's interpretation was the same adopted by the American authors of the Declaration of Independence who, like him, placed responsibility for the separation of the colonies from Britain squarely upon King George's "fatal ambition" and "partial and selfish views." Such is the so-called Whig opinion of the reign of George III, familiar to Americans as the traditional interpretation of the revolution, of which it is an integral part: King George ascended the throne with the fixed intention of overthrowing English constitutional liberty and of restoring the prerogative to its former high position. In this attempt he was steadily supported by the Scots and Tories, and resisted as steadily by the Whigs. The attempt to subject the colonies to the crown was part of this insidious scheme. Nevertheless, the king finally failed because of the assistance which the Whigs in America gave to their brethren in England. Thus English patriots vanquished their king at Yorktown, Virginia. This view certainly flatters American national pride. Whether myth or Gothic romance or fact, this Whig interpretation of history came to be accepted as true. Certainly, at the time it was extremely plausible to many political observers.[15]

In the voluminous *Last Journals,* Walpole concludes his narrative of British political history in his own time.[16] Only in a very few places is the work rough and unfinished, Walpole not having the time or the inclination to rewrite and polish all his memoranda. Generally, these journals are not noticeably unlike the preceding memoirs, except for fewer formal "characters" of the chief personages and interpretive essays or reviews of historical events. Such essays required care, which may also explain why Walpole did not quite complete these papers.

With regard to the public address of the parliamentarians, Walpole admitted that he had "given very inadequate ideas of the speeches of Burke, Charles Fox, and Wedderburn, three excellent orators in different ways." He continued: "I could only relate what I heard at secondhand, or from notes communicated to me, which must be imperfect when not taken in shorthand" (I, 70).[17] But his informants in Parliament proved to be indefatigable, for much space is given to debates, Walpole's interest in address and argument persisting to the end. Occasionally, Walpole was also present himself. For example, as he wrote (April 7, 1772), he learned of a new political luminary: "Though I had never been in the House of Commons since I had quitted Parliament, the fame of Charles Fox raised my curiosity, and I went this day to hear him" (I, 80). Then he proceeds with an analysis of the ideas and a comparison of the styles of several speakers, including Fox and Burke (I, 81).

The major debates recorded by Walpole were those on the Royal Marriage Bill in 1772, India and Lord Clive (he thought of Clive as an imperialist plunderer and called him a "great criminal" [I, 231]), the momentous issue of the American War, and parliamentary and administrative reform. The journal was kept up to September, 1783, when the Peace of Paris concluded the war, which, in its last few years, involved France, Spain, and Holland, as well as the United Provinces and Britain. After Lord North's long ministry was dissolved, another government in March, 1782, under Rockingham and Shelburne was formed to settle the treaty. But upon the death of Rockingham three months later, there was a good deal of confusion. After Shelburne's fall, a coalition in April, 1783, under Fox and North was formed, and then another under Lord John Cavendish and the duke of Portland before that of William Pitt the younger in December, 1783. Walpole, representing the older generation, did not know quite how to read the instability of the times; in 1783 the old party labels appeared to him to be losing their usefulness: "all parties were so jumbled and so prostituted, that no shadow of principles remained in any party; nor could any man say which faction was Whig or Tory. The Crown was humbled and disgraced—the people were sold; a coalition of potent chiefs had seized power, yet could not be called the aristocracy, for the Peers were divided too" (II, 518).

Walpole was clearly aware of the coming of new figures on the historical scene, Charles Fox and William Pitt, the young sons of the leaders in Walpole's generation; but he was uncertain of the principles they upheld, uncertain of directions: "new struggles must give new and separate distinctions, and some time probably will pass before either of the three constituent parts of the Legislature will preponderate eminently" (II, 518). Soon, however, he contradicted himself. For, as he returned to his major theme—the conflict between tyranny and liberty, king and Parliament—he was able to give some meaning to the history of the last ten years: "Had the American war been prosperous, I have no doubt but the power of the Crown would have swelled to most dangerous heights. Its miscarriage has compensated to the country by the diminution of the Crown's influence. It even is deprived, *at present*, of the choice of its Ministers" (II, 521—22). Clearly, he was looking in the right direction, toward parliamentary supremacy and an extremely limited monarchy.

As we have already seen, Walpole's major theme deals with the king's excessive assertion of his prerogative. In these journals the king's desire for more power than was warranted by the constitution was exposed on numerous occasions. For example, the king wished to protect the purity of the blood royal by restricting marriages between members of his family and English subjects. Walpole, interested personally as well as ideologically, thereupon reported in detail the speeches on the Royal Marriage Bill (1772). At first, because of his prejudice against monarchy, Walpole objected to the marriage of his niece, Maria Walpole, to the duke of Gloucester, a prince of the blood. Eventually, however, as a result of the king's wish to see this bill passed, the king's opposition to this marriage and his persecution of the duke's family, Walpole came to her side.

The king's failure to recognize the marriage, he condemned as cruel and brutal (I, 207); and he was bitter at the king's "pride, ill-nature, duplicity, and pusillanimity" (I, 226) as he noted the devious ways the monarch forced high society to ostracize the duke and his wife. Thus Walpole thought this bill unjust (as it gave King George the right to interfere in the private lives of his whole family), potentially productive of civil wars, and clear evidence of an illegal and unconstitutional "extension of prerogative" (I, 47, 52). His friend Conway, again threatened with loss of place by voting against the king, came to Walpole for advice. No doubt aroused by his strong feeling against wrong, Walpole broke his promise to himself not to interfere in Conway's political life should crucial issues arise. He begged Conway "not to recant"; he begged him to hold fast to his principles and preserve his honor at whatever cost to his income: "The question, I said, was indeed personal to the King—nay, and too personal, for it went to an extension of his prerogative, a point in which he ought not to ask or expect to be obliged. That the duty to our country was to supersede private gratitude. Kings might enslave a nation if their favours were to tie men up from obliging their conscience" (I, 52). Conway followed his advice. Still, despite strong opposition, the bill passed and the ruler had his way.

The theme of liberty is most significantly expressed in the extended narrative of the difficult relationship between the American colonies and the mother country. When the news of the Boston Tea Party reached London in January, 1774, initiating a protracted series of bitter debates over the punishment of Massachusetts, "the era of the American War," as Walpole called it, was begun (I, 312n.). That Parliament refused to hear the Americans irritated him. In May, 1774, after an American petition was neglected by Parliament, Walpole declared that "Insolence was now the language of the Court," and he also accused it of despotic measures threatening violence against any who supported the Americans (I, 338), soon called "English rebels" by the king (II, 149).

When in the same month the Quebec Bill was passed, giving toleration to Canadian Roman Catholics, he wrote, "Parliament was now the instrument of despotism. A bill of so Stuart a complexion," one "that establishes Popery," was to him obviously poorly timed; it was "another remarkable event in the American quarrel": "An hundred thousand Catholics in Canada were a good resource for the Crown against the independence affected by the protestant colonies" (I, 344, 354, 357). He is amazed and furious to learn that the bishops supported the punitive measures against Boston, "those cruel bills," and that they "made no objections to the indulgences shown to the Roman Catholics in Quebec!" (I, 346). From the point of view of the Anglican bishops, Walpole said ironically, the conflict "became a religious war against Dissenters" (I, 357). In general, his attitude toward the British clergy during the American war was invariably unflattering. The following quotation is typical of his hostility: "On the bill for preventing abuse of Sunday, Lord Abingdon made a bitter and well-deserved invective on the bishops for their hypocrisy, and for their bloody votes on the American war" (II, 365). Indeed, in June, 1774, when Walpole felt that hope for a peaceful solution to the American problem was negligible, his agonized fears for liberty were so appalling that he could scarcely write:

This nation has had many escapes: Heaven can work them for us when there is no prospect. O Liberty, thou first of blessings, may Heaven preserve thee in this almost only country in which thou dost exist! Shall a Prince whose family was brought hither to defend thee—shall servile Peers, venal Members of Parliament, and Bishops . . . sacrifice thee and their posterity for titles and pay that are equally a reproach to them? . . . the prospect so gloomy, I am almost tempted to burn my pen and discontinue my Journal—I will continue it in hopes of better days. (I, 358)

In November, 1774, he reported that "the Court agents were going all lengths in inflaming the nation against the Americans and reviving all the old exploded doctrines of the Stuarts" (I, 410). Thus in the new Parliament, "the current ran strongly against the Americans," for it was even "more submissive than the last" to the wishes of the monarch (I, 412). The king was so uncompromising (I, 413) and "the Court had worked up both the Parliament and the people to such a frenzy for the supremacy over America" (I, 436) that conflict was made inevitable. Indeed, according to Walpole's "hypothesis," as he described his explanation of the motivating forces behind the events that led to war, George III and his secret junto of confidential ministers, Lord Mansfield and Charles Jenkinson, and possibly a few others, intended to drive "all or many of the colonies into rebellion" (I, 415). In February, 1775, when the policy of the administration was supported by the "corrupt and servile" majority, Walpole interpreted the result as *"a vote for a civil war,"* italicized words that his footnote explained as marking the "Commencement of the war" (I, 429). And when on May 28, 1775, news of the actual opening of hostilities at Lexington and Concord reached London, he had only high praise for the rebels: "The provincials had behaved with the greatest conduct, coolness, and resolution," which "spoke a thorough determination of resistance" (I, 464).

After the severe British losses at Bunker Hill, and the investment of their army in Boston, Walpole declared "the Ministers now saw America was lost, or not to be recovered but by long time and vast expense; yet, not daring to own their miscarriage, pushed on" (I, 471). The Americans, however, again behaved admirably (I, 477), and their early successes cheered him: "I had almost despaired of liberty. At least now [October, 1775] it did not seem in great danger in America" (I, 481). At this time, too, an attempt was made to bribe Walpole by means of making the sinecure in the Custom House which he shared with his brother his own for life; but he proved incorruptible: "It was not probable that at fifty-eight I would disgrace my whole life, character, and principles, for a lucrative offer that I could flatter myself with few years' enjoyment of . . . " (I, 489).

The opposition divided and lacking leadership, Walpole became very pessimistic for the future of his country (I, 498–99, 512). At the beginning of the new year, January, 1776, he was unable to rouse the outspoken and pro-American Duke of Richmond, who was much too delicate, too refined and honorable, to provoke debate with the teasing motions which Walpole proposed. As for the leaders of the majority, they were vicious and reactionary, and the king was a rank Tory Jacobite (I, 513–14). Even the Anglican bishops and clergy, he raged almost hysterically, stood "ready to profit by the restoration of Stuart views. How deeply and joyfully they waded into a civil war on the Constitution and on Dissenters, let their votes, addresses, and zeal for the war declare!" (I, 514). Moreover, the Presbyterians and Dissenters, he wrote in disgust, "who could not but see . . . the notorious partiality of the Court to Roman Catholics, were entirely passive in England, being bribed or sold by their leaders" (I, 588). By the end of 1776, he noted that the whole country had turned against the opposition.

Walpole followed the war in detail. Checking on all the newspapers kept him well informed on the events and battles overseas. In sum, from his point of view the American war was from the first unwise, unnecessary, and criminally vicious; and when fought, it was led ineptly and supplied poorly. He thought British defeat was inevitable; yet at the same time he often despaired of the possibility of an American victory (June, 1776; I, 561). Walpole simply could not credit any news of British victories; he was always searching for and finding contradictory reports, always suspecting that the court party was suppressing bad news of colonial victories. Eventually, when Burgoyne's army surren-

dered at Saratoga in October, 1777, the opposition became confident
and demanded peace; but, as usual, it was voted down. To illustrate the
difficulty faced by Walpole's friends, the pathetic admission by the
famous historian Edward Gibbon may be cited: Gibbon sadly avowed
to Walpole in November, 1777, "that if it had not been for shame,
there were not twenty men in the House but were ready to vote for
peace. I did not think it very decent in so sensible a man to support the
war, and make such a confession" (II, 76).[18]. Thus, even after the loss
of Burgoyne's whole army, George and his supporters obstinately
persisted in carrying on, despite the fact that everyone knew the war
was going badly and the cause practically hopeless (January, 1778; II,
89).

The rest belongs to history. Soon came the defeat at Yorktown of
Cornwallis by General Washington and the French Admiral D'Estaing in
November, 1781, followed by the definitive treaty of the Peace of Paris
in September, 1783. The bad news of Yorktown, Walpole wrote, threw
the court and administration "into great confusion and distress" (II,
378). Although the American war was "rendered hopeless, yet the
King," he reported with indignation in January, 1782, "was not in the
least more inclined to give it up" (II, 395); and, despite the fact that
the end was inevitable, the king had many stubborn supporters in the
House of Commons who also could not admit defeat. It is interesting to
note that Conway who "invariably lamented the American war" (II,
406), and had moved the repeal of the Stamp Act more than fifteen
years before, also moved for peace on February 20, 1782. At first his
motion was defeated by a vote of 194 to 193! A week later, however,
he tried again and succeeded in carrying his motion by a vote of 234 to
215, bringing to an end what Walpole called "so fatal a war, and so
impotent and shameful an Administration" (II, 410–11). Thus,
Walpole grimly repeated after Charles Fox that Conway had twice saved
his country (II, 451–52). But George III, "by grasping at
despotism . . . lost more dominions than every monarch lost who did
not lose his crown" (II, 418–19, 476, 533).

What should be done to those responsible for this debacle? In
accordance with his basic political norm, Walpole wished "to see the
constitution restored, and the arbitrary spirit of the King and Junto
punished. To me," he confessed, "it would be preferable to have the
nation humbled, provided it remained free, than to see it victorious and
enslaved" (II, 147). While he did not wish to go so far as capital
punishment, he hoped the new ministry would impose "stigmatizing
censures and fines" on the late ministry: "the latter would deter men in

future from exerting too much alacrity in enlarging the prerogative, and the former would make it much more difficult for the Crown to recall its disgraced tools" (II, 430).

Walpole also asked for a gradual decrease of the royal power (II, 419); and this did occur, Walpole was pleased to note, but only as a part of the historical process, not as a penalty. His advice was not taken. Still, he was happy to see Conway appointed to the command of the army, "the centre of my wishes" (II, 431), because with "the bravest, coolest, most constitutional General at the head" the king could not "establish absolute power by the army" (II, 432). He had already made the point that by December, 1778, although Britain could not win in America, it had three hundred thousand men under arms, "the greatest military establishment ever kept up in Europe, except by Louis XIV at the period of his greatest power" (II, 226). Thus we can understand his apprehension: "Had the conquest of America been achieved, I have not the smallest doubt but a triumphant army, returned from subduing the King's enemies, and stigmatized by the Americans as Tories, would have been unbounded, being ready to make war on all called Whigs, and all the King should call his enemies" (March, 1782, II, 432; also March, 1778, II, 147–49).[19]

Walpole is absolutely consistent in his opinion about the menace of monarchy. He did not have to seek confirmation for his Whig views about the despotic tendencies of George III in any of Burke's writings. Thoroughly Whig, Walpole never altered his antipathy to Tories and kings. But, on the other hand, he did not want kings destroyed; he did not believe in Tom Paine's democratic leveling (to Mary Berry, April 3, 1791). In the period of the French Revolution, which was soon to come, he may properly be called, as we have said before, an Old Whig.

CHAPTER 3

The Connoisseur and Art Critic

I *Houghton Hall:* Aedes Walpolianae

HORACE WALPOLE'S taste, initially developed at Houghton Hall, was refined by his Grand Tour visits to art galleries and by his irrepressible collector's zeal. But Houghton Hall, begun by his father Sir Robert in 1722 and completed in 1735, was all important as a fundamental formative influence upon his critical sense. The reason is easy to see upon examination of Walpole's first catalogue and first important literary work done when he was a young man, *Aedes Walpolianae [The House of the Walpoles],* or *A Description of the Collection of Pictures at Houghton-Hall in Norfolk* (written in 1742–43, published in 1747), illustrated with engravings by George Vertue.

For example, we learn that his later admiration for William Kent, expressed in the essay "On Modern Gardening," as well as his understanding of Kent's limitations as a painter, was grounded on his familiarity with this artist's work at Houghton. The catalogue indicates that Kent decorated the walls of the great staircase in chiaroscuro, painted the ceiling of the saloon, and designed all the ornaments or furnishings throughout the house. We learn, too, that not only was his father a great collector but that his mother was a collector of sorts. She filled a glass case "with a large quantity of silver philegree."[1] Apparently, because Walpole had just the right temperament, as well as the intelligence to be benefited by Houghton, the result of such conditioning was almost inevitable—an easy familiarity with great works of art, and a desire to catalogue and to criticize the works of artists, culminating in the huge compendium *Anecdotes of Painting* (including *A Catalogue of Engravers*). All in all, Houghton, with its fabulous collections and its luxurious decorations, formed his taste at the same time that it stimulated interest in minutiae and antiquarian researches for accurate and authenticated information about art and artists.

The *Aedes* was prepared, as Walpole says in his introduction, on the model of the famous Italian collections described in the *Aedes Barbarinae* and *Giustinianae*. It includes an essay distinguishing the characteristics of the several schools of European art of interest to English connoisseurs in the mid-eighteenth century, a few plates illustrating the plan and appearance of Houghton, a detailed room-by-room inventory of the works of virtu to be seen, and a sermon on painting. In a sense, his is a work engendered by pride; for Walpole advertises to the world that his father had gathered at Houghton Hall a collection of art rivaling the best in Italy, "the native soil of almost all virtu" (II, 225). There is no question but that his pride was justified.

Houghton itself is a miniature palace, "a House of State and Conveniency, and, in some degree, worthy of the great and generous Patron," writes the architect Colen Campbell in his *Vitruvius Britannicus* (1715–25).[2] The house is grand, plain, massive; but elegance is suggested by low-built pavilions on either side and by colonnades that curve gracefully to them from the main house. As Campbell indicates in his general plan, the front and offices on each side extend four hundred and fifty feet. The front to the great entrance lying open to the park extends one hundred and sixty-six feet. The exterior decoration is Classical, with domed towers and lantern cupolas of stone, urns and statues and a Palladian railing decorating the roof line of the central house. The east front entrance is surmounted by reclining figures of Neptune and Britannia by Michael Rysbrack. The lines are severe, so that the dominant effect of the noble structure is dignity and grandeur, achieving a monumental unity and splendor truly Palladian.

West of the house were twenty-three acres of a garden laid out by "Mr. Eyre, an imitator" of the famous landscape gardener Charles Bridgman, and "then reckoned a considerable portion," according to Walpole himself.[3] The layout of plantation and grove resulted in a stately park, "very large and beautiful," wrote Campbell. Even today the extensive vistas down long avenues leading from the house, and the vast lawn before the west front (contained by a haha), are still impressive. In 1720, the design of the grounds was one of the first attempts at a somewhat natural landscape setting for a house, certainly of some significance to one who was soon to become the leading exponent of the informal or English garden.

In his essay on gardening, Walpole commended Bridgman, whose disciple Eyre designed the layout of the garden at Houghton, as the first to deviate from a rigid symmetrical plan and to offer "even morsels of a forest appearance": "though he still adhered much to straight walks with high clipped hedges, they were only his great lines; the rest he diversified by wilderness, and with loose groves of oak, though still within surrounding hedges." However, Walpole also credited Bridgman with "the invention of fosses," or hahas, the sunken fence that, taking the place of walls, permitted an unobstructed vista. Houghton, according to Walpole, was "one of the first gardens planted in this simple though still formal style."[4]

"Within, there is no austerity but a riot of luxurious decoration," says J. H. Plumb.[5] Embellished sumptuously and lavishly—marble chimney pieces and figures over doors by Rysbrack (in the marble parlor and in the hall), furniture by Kent, richly gilt mirrors, elaborate plaster work, beautifully carved doorcases and carefully hung doors and staircase balustrades in expensive mahogany, then newly introduced—Houghton Hall had all sorts of decoration that were the result of the most careful craftsmanship. There was even a "fine pear-tree carving" by Grinling Gibbons over the chimney of the common parlor, and a frame carving, gilt, by Gibbons over the chimney in the drawing room. At this time, Gibbons was probably the best wood carver in all of Europe. The great hall, "a cube of forty [feet]," was decorated with friezes by Rysbrack over the doors and with busts, heads, and vases, antique and modern. The frieze in the huge gallery was taken from the Sibyl's Temple at Hadrian's Villa at Tivoli.[6]

Visiting Houghton Hall in 1739, George Vertue, who was commissioned by Sir Robert to purchase paintings and by Horace to provide prints for the *Aedes,* made this entry in his journal: "The Magnificence and beauty of this structure being well known . . . the range of the State Rooms being all finely adorned and furnished with great Variety rich furniture carving Gilding Marble and Stucco works—every room in a different manner." Such are a few of the details of the interior—truly an appropriately splendid setting for the finest collection of paintings in England in the early eighteenth century; and so Vertue continues his account: "but the great Collection of noble original pictures exceed all others in numbers and variety. . . . So many rare pictures, statues, requires time to view well and review at several times to conceive their great merit and beauty."[7] The cost of the house must have been stupendous; with the art collection, it was simply priceless.

By 1736, when Horace was about nineteen years old, Sir Robert possessed over four hundred paintings—large and small masterpieces by a host of great artists. Every important school, according to Walpole's classification, was represented by the following artists among others: the English by Charles Jervas (5), Jonathan Richardson (1), Godfrey Kneller (8); the Flemish by Peter Paul Rubens (11), including two large canvases of Susanna and the Elders and Mary Magdalen Washing Christ's Feet, Anthony Vandyck (14), Rembrandt (2), David Teniers (4), Hans Holbein (1), a portrait of Erasmus; the French by Nicolo Poussin (3), Gaspar Poussin (4), Claude Lorrain (2); the Spanish by Bartolomé Murillo (5) and Diego Velasquez (2); the Venetian by Paul Veronese (3) and Titian (2); the Milanese by Da Vinci (1); the Florentine by Andrea del Sarto (1); the Roman by Raphael (2), Michael Angelo (1), and Carlo Maratti (13); the Neapolitan by Salvatore Rosa (4), including the Prodigal Son; and the Bolognese by Annibal Caracci (3), Francesco Albano (2), Domenichino (1), and Guido Reni (5), including a "capital picture, the first in this collection, the Doctors of the Church" (II, 266).

Only superlatives can adequately describe such a collection. As Walpole says, not without justification, "There are not a great many collections left in Italy more worth seeing than this at Houghton: in the preservation of the pictures, it certainly excells most of them." The Italian paintings are far more numerous and varied than the others, and so the masters of the several Italian schools receive most of his attention and the greatest praise. But, as there were quite a few famous artists representing other countries, he could also add truthfully that "there are enough here for any man who studies painting to form very true ideas of most of the chief schools and to acquaint himself with most of the chief hands" (II, 226).

After briefly discussing the origin of painting among the ancients, he proceeds in the *Aedes* to range through the various schools, and confidently, almost arrogantly, to discriminate them and to praise and blame like an experienced and sophisticated connoisseur. Concerning the Flemish, "those drudging mimicks of nature's most uncomely coarsenesses," he objects to their low subjects. However, he excepts Rubens "who struck out of the littlenesses of his countrymen, though he never fell into a character of graceful beauty" (II, 226). He makes no comment on Rembrandt. He pays homage to Gaspar Poussin and Claude Lorrain, "in their way the greatest ornaments to their profession . . . the latter especially was the Raphael of landscape-painting" (II, 234).

Salvator Rosa, the Neapolitan who resided in Rome, he singled out as a great genius capable of producing a painting which had "majesty of thought equal to Raphael, an expression great as Poussin's": "His thoughts, his expression, his landscapes, his knowledge of the force of shade, and his masterly arrangement of horror and distress, have placed him in the first class of painters" (II, 233). His lengthy tribute to Salvator, even including a comparison with Shakespeare, is typically extravagant for the time.

Occasionally, Walpole stops to explain details in paintings—pointing out typically "Romish" anachronisms or giving a brief history of the subject, thereby revealing his learning. Finally, he rapidly recapitulates the faults and virtues of the masters and concludes, with the air of an expert, "in my opinion, all the qualities of a perfect painter never met but in Raphael, Guido [Reni], and Annibal Caracci." It is curious that this introductory survey has nothing to say about the English school, and Walpole suggests by its omission, or oversight, the relative unimportance of these artists in early eighteenty-century English collections.

In essence, the *Aedes Walpolianiae* is a monument to Sir Robert Walpole, a son's way of honoring his father. The young man's high regard for his famous father may also be seen in his sermon on painting, which was preached at Houghton in 1742 (II, 279—87). Here Horace lashes out at Roman Catholic superstition, particularly, and in view of his subject and the large collection of Italian religious paintings, he warns against the Romish practice of worshiping images rather than the real and living God of nature. The study of painting, he declares, must lead to knowledge of the creator: "Then were painting united with devotion, and ransomed from idolatry; and the blended labours of the preacher and painter might lend to the glory of God." He is indignant at the impious corruption of painting "to the mercenary purposes of priestly ambition," including those of the Pope.

On the other hand, he righteously claims that painting in England serves a useful moral purpose in memorializing the good works of King William, who "flew to save religion and liberty," and the honesty and benevolence of George of Hanover. Moreover, paintings illustrating biblical parables serve a moral purpose, he believes, far more effectively than the example of "the Romish saints" (II, 282, 284—85). Because of all the religious paintings from Italy in the Houghton collection, this compulsion to attack Catholic idolatry—"droning monks," "churlish recluseness," "bloody Dominican" are some examples of his severity—is both amusing and embarrassing.

Having in mind his father's recent forced resignation as prime minister, Horace concludes with allegorical remarks on Sir Robert as the unrewarded Moses, the "slighted patriot," who preserved Israel. If we place all these harsh religious and political comments in the context of anti-Jacobitism, of a Whig satire on the treacherous Tories for "a dogmatical defence of church prerogatives" (II, 286), and of Whig fears of what the Pretender's son might do next—fears which were at the heart of Robert Walpole's policy of strengthening the Protestant succession and which were in a few years to materialize in an invasion from France—then perhaps we can understand the ungenerous party-minded spirit in which they were made. The sermon thus gives a politico-religious interpretation and vindication of the prime minister's connoisseurship.

In the little bed-chamber of Houghton, two portraits faced each other, one by Michael Dahl of Catherine Shorter, Robert Walpole's first wife and Horace's mother; and another by John Vanloo of Maria Skerritt, Sir Robert's second wife (II, 246). Similarly, in the great parlor, or refectory, of Strawberry Hill were original portraits and copies by John Giles Eckhardt of members of Horace Walpole's whole family, including his father, mother, and Maria Skerritt.[8] Their presence at Houghton and at Strawberry Hill suggests the respect and dignity which his elders were accorded by Horace Walpole throughout his life. The young son may have felt deeply the loss of his mother in 1737; but Horace clearly held no grudge against his father for marrying his mistress, Miss Skerritt, the year after. Such may be the meaning of Houghton to the boy and young man Horace Walpole. He loved and respected his father—and, even before his visits to art galleries abroad, he could express, in his letter of July 27, 1736, to his father, his appreciation of what Sir Robert had accomplished: "As fine as Houghton is, I shou'd not have felt half the satisfaction, if it had not been your doing: I wish all your other Actions cou'd afford you as much ease to enjoy their Success, as those at Houghton do: But as I know how little leisure you have, I will not detain you by endeavouring to express in a long letter, what the Longest cou'd never do, my Duty and Admiration."

The immense cost of Houghton must have taxed even Sir Robert's income. In 1745, after his father had died, Horace wrote to Mann (April 15, 1745), "It is certain he is dead very poor: his debts . . . amount to £50,000. His estate, a nominal £8,000 a year, much mortgaged. In short, his fondness for Houghton had endangered Houghton." As a result of his extravagance, Sir Robert made it difficult for his heirs to carry on. The third earl of Orford, Horace's nephew George Walpole, who inherited the estate in 1751, was particularly incompetent. In the middle of 1773, when the earl had become temporarily insane, Walpole had to spend a disagreeable fortnight at Houghton in order to take care of his nephew's affairs—to effect drastic economies and reforms so that the estate might be saved. He told Henry Conway and Lady Ossory (August 30 and September 1, 1773) that, although almost everything else was in ruin, "the pictures, the glorious pictures," were "in the finest preservation."

Later in 1779, George Walpole's wanton extravagance continuing, and after he recovered from his second mental illness, he sold the art treasures for about £40,000 to the Czarina Catherine of Russia, where they formed the basis of the Hermitage collection. Walpole could do nothing to prevent the sale. Shocked and horrified, he exclaimed angrily to Mann on August 4, 1779, "Well! adieu to Houghton! about its mad master I shall never trouble myself more." Anger soon gave way to grief: "It is the most signal mortification to my idolatry for my father's memory that I could receive," he lamented in a letter of great poignancy to Bentley on September 18, 1779; "It is stripping the temple of his glory and of his affection. A madman excited by rascals has burnt his Ephesus."

The setting of Houghton exerted in many ways a determining influence on the boy and young man Horace Walpole. For one, it gave him self-identity, as it brought father and son close together in an intimacy that had never been achieved before. Thus, its psychological significance was of fundamental importance, for it made possible balance and stability, purpose and direction. After his father's death in 1745, and after launching his own career, Walpole could only parody his father's achievement—in politics and art. In politics, he could not be prime minister, but he could be the man behind him, as he was when his closest friend Henry Conway became leader of the House of Commons; in art, he could not afford a palatial country house, but he could build by degrees his "toy" castle; nor could he afford expensive oil paintings by the old masters, but he did have the best collection in England of miniatures, prints, and drawings, especially printed heads. He had, for example, three hundred of Albrecht Dürer's prints, two hundred and forty of Caracci's, hundreds of William Faithorne's and Wenceslauf Hollar's, and the most extensive collection of William Hogarth ever made. He also had more than ten thousand English "Heads" from Alfred the Great to George III: and he thought he owned the finest enameled miniature in the world—Christian Frederick Zincke's miniature of Abraham Cowley.[9]

Even the semi-naturalistic garden at Houghton, with its haha and its irregular plantings that gave "a forest appearance," exerted an influence. After a visit to the place, he wrote to his friend Lyttleton (July 27, 1736), "I spent my time at Houghton for the first week almost alone; we have a charming garden all wilderness; much adapted to my romantic inclinations." This "wilderness" was deliberately planned, according to Charles Bridgman's ideas, as part of the total garden; undoubtedly it was impressed on Walpole's subconscious mind, nurturing his romantic inclinations at the time he designed and planted his own little asymmetrical garden at Strawberry Hill. And, of course, Walpole's garden also had a haha that permitted an unobstructed view of the Thames from the house.

There may even be a relationship between Houghton and his sole tragedy, *The Mysterious Mother.* It is curiously pathetic to see in his wonderful letter to his friend Montagu (March 25–30, 1761), a long and poignant reverie on Houghton as he had once known it when controlled by his father, how after a sixteen-year interval he slipped into the position of his father (although not yet bearer of the title), and how, perhaps, identification with his father may have contributed to the remorse and atonement of Edmund which he dramatized in the play. Edmund, it will be remembered, also returns to his ancestral home after sixteen years! Sadly, unconsciously, as he expresses his feelings to Montagu, Walpole assumes the role of his father, choosing to sleep in his father's little dressing room, which is adjacent to his mother's bedchamber, and to write on his father's escritoire. The parody of Sir Robert is painfully obvious in Walpole's ritualistic Oedipal behavior.

Houghton also gave Walpole a visual frame through which he saw life and from which he developed certain well-defined expectations. The grand scale of the house and grounds, the splendor of the interior decorations, and the art treasures, must have inspired in him a sense of greatness, a profound sense of the meaning of his social position backed by the wealth and power in which his father had gloried. "The outstanding mansion of the Whig oligarchy," as it had been called by Christopher Hussey,[10] Houghton Hall made clear to Walpole that spiritually and materially he belonged to the nobility, and that he expected the class to which he belonged to rule Britain.

In all these ways, then, Houghton determined Horace Walpole's psychological attitude and his ideological principles. But with regard to taste and virtu, finally, it is also clear that Walpole's antiquarian inclinations, which generally always turned on art, were formed at

Houghton. These are expressed not only in his own house, Strawberry Hill, but also in the art collections he maintained there, and his learned history of art in England, *Anecdotes of Painting.*

When his nephew, the third earl of Orford, died in 1791 without a legitimate heir, Walpole was bequeathed the whole of the Norfolk estates. They were heavily encumbered; and the main building at Houghton was in a terrible state of disrepair, even the flight of steps which rose to the *piano nobile* having been given away. Walpole, who thought of himself as "the poorest Earl in England," knew he could do very little for the neglected property, yet he felt spiritually at rest. As he wrote to Lady Ossory (December 10, 1791), "I will just say that I am perfectly content"; [my nephew] "has restored me to my birthright, and I shall call myself obliged to him, and be grateful to his memory." Although it belonged to him at last, he never did inhabit the palace of Houghton Hall in the few years that remained to him. But upon his death on March 2, 1797, at the age of eighty, Horace Walpole was interred with his family in the little church on the Houghton estate; and with him concluded the male line of the descendants of Sir Robert Walpole.

II   *Gothic Architect:* A Description of Strawberry Hill

On June 5, 1747, Walpole told Conway that he had leased "a little plaything house . . . and . . . the prettiest bauble you ever saw" on the left bank of the Thames not far from Pope's Villa in Twickenham, at that time a lovely suburb of London. It was located in a picturesque spot, as he wrote enthusiastically to Horace Mann on the same day: "the prospect is as delightful as possible, commanding the river, the town, and Richmond Park; and being situated on a hill descends to the Thames through two or three little meadows, where I have some Turkish sheep and two cows, all studied in their colours for becoming the view."

He found the rural scene picturesque and charming; but, as it turned out, he had another reason for choosing Twickenham for his home in the country. To one sensitive not only to innovation but also to historical tradition and very much alive to the meaning of place, it was an ideal location with many significant associations. Colley Cibber, for example, was one of the first tenants of his new home; and, as he later recorded in his verse "The Parish Register of Twickenham" (c. 1758), the earl of Essex, Bacon, Lord Clarendon, Lady Mary Wortley Montagu,

Henry Fielding, the earl of Chesterfield, as well as Pope had resided in the area:

> Where Pope in moral music spoke
> To th'anguish'd soul of Bolingbroke,
> And whisper'd, how true genius errs,
> Preferring joys that pow'r confers;
> Bliss, never to great minds arising
> From ruling worlds, but from despising.[11]

In 1748, Walpole purchased the property. Looking over some old deeds, Walpole learned that "the name Strawberry-hill was not, as some suppose, a modern application. In the old leases it is named Strawberry-hill Shot. The house was built by a nobleman's coach-man for a lodging house; and some people of rank lived in it before it came to me."[12] So he writes to Mann in June, 1748, "You shall hear from me from Strawberry Hill, which I have found out in my lease is the old name of my house; so pray, never call it Twickenham again." At the end of the year, he added nine acres to the original five, thereby giving himself ample grounds for planting and landscaping, for gardening like an English gentleman. (He continued to make further purchases of land during the next forty years, so that at the time of his death in 1797, his estate comprised nearly forty-seven acres, at a total cost of about £4000.)[13] He had an extensive lawn, for which the grounds were famous, "a terrace the whole breadth of his garden on the brow of a natural hill, with meadows at the foot, and commanding the river, the village [Twickenham], Richmond-hill, and the park, and part of Kingston" (to Mann, December 26, 1748).

So, as Walpole at the age of thirty leased, purchased, and began to improve Strawberry Hill, his life achieved a certain cultural focus. At this time, Walpole was engaged mainly in three activities: he participated in politics and wrote political memoirs; he described contemporary life and chronicled significant social and political events in his letters; and he developed his taste for antiquities and virtu— collecting old relics and *objets d'art*. These activities now largely centered on one master passion—the Gothicizing of Strawberry Hill, his humble dwelling in the country that grew to become one of the most famous houses in the kingdom.

After laying out the grounds and planting, Walpole was in the mood to work on the house itself. In September, 1749, after his first antiquarian tour in Sussex, he had his first thoughts of reconstructing his home and transforming it into a miniature Gothic castle with

pointed arches, old stained-glass, arched and quartrefoil windows, a
tower, battlements, and pinnacles (to Montagu, August 20 and
September 28, 1749). On January 10, 1750, he asked Mann, who was
in Italy, for some assistance: "I am going to build a little Gothic castle
at Strawberry Hill. If you can pick me up any fragments of old painted
glass, arms, or anything, I shall be excessively obliged to you."

Mann objected to the Gothic craze. Still, Walpole persisted, despite
the unfashionable parvenu taste for Gothic, which at this time
permeated domestic architecture and interior decoration—furniture,
wallpaper, window frames, fireplaces, gateways with pinnacles, and
landscapes with Gothic hermitages and grottoes. He was glad, he wrote
Mann on April 27, 1753, to imprint "the gloomth of abbeys and
cathedrals" on his house. Even William Whitehead, in Walpole's favorite
journal, *The World* (March 22, 1753), satirized the vulgar indiscretions
of Gothic taste and indicated that approved taste had shifted to
chinoiserie. But Walpole was unaffected by the Chinese vogue. Also, he
deliberately rejected the Palladian neo-Greek style for his remodeling
because he wanted something irregular:

The Grecian, [he rationalized,] was only proper for magnificent and
public buildings. Columns and all their beautiful ornaments, look
ridiculous when crowded into a closet or a cheesecake-house. The
variety is little, and admits no charming irregularities. I am almost as
fond of the Sharawaggi [*sic*], or Chinese want of symmetry, in
buildings, as in grounds or gardens. I am sure, whenever you come to
England, you will be pleased with the liberty of taste into which we are
struck, and of which you can have no idea. (To Mann, January 10,
1750)

Once, however, when he visited Mereworth Castle, Kent, he confessed
to Bentley on August 7, 1752, that the perfection of its Palladianism
weaned him from Gothicism; but his disloyalty was only temporary.

Walpole did first think of renovating Strawberry Hill in other
styles—Venetian or Mosque Gothic and the Chinese Sharawadgi; but
these were never considered seriously, and so he soon resolved on the
"charming and venerable Gothic." Houghton, too, it must be
remembered, was in the predominant symmetrical and serene Palladian
style; and, of course, he could not simply reduplicate his father's efforts
if his objective were to assert his own ego. Besides, Houghton,
compared with the original cheesecake Strawberry Hill, was an
enormous magnificent structure on the grand scale, and it was in the
possession of Walpole's eldest brother. Walpole wanted something more
dynamic and exciting.

Perhaps his chief reason for choosing Gothic over the only seriously competing style, the Classical, was romantic enthusiasm. As he wrote in his *Anecdotes of Painting,* "One must have taste to be sensible of the beauties of Grecian architecture; one only wants passions to feel Gothic."[14] He refers to "a *magic* hardiness in the execution" of some Gothic works; and in the last paragraph of his *Description of Strawberry Hill* he also refers to "the romantic caste of the mansion," as a special quality that should "raise pleasing sensations." Obviously, the affective quality of Gothic was a significant factor. But other reasons also made Gothic his inevitable choice. England had many evidences of Gothic remains—ruined monasteries, churches, and castles; and Walpole, fascinated by medieval antiquarianism, had just taken the first of his many Gothic tours with his friend John Chute. He was also interested in his family's past, in genealogy particularly, and thus in the buildings of his ancestors. Family pride, combined with nationalism, therefore, provided a powerful sentimental motivation.

Then, again, his formative years at Cambridge must have been more influential than he had realized at the time. As his poem on Henry VI's architectural triumph demonstrates, he admired King's College Chapel—and certainly its exquisite fan-vaulting inspired his attempt at duplication in the gallery, the best room in his villa.[15] Moreover, the Gothic spirit of the great court, the chapel and gateways of Trinity College nearby, must have permeated his unconscious; for, as he later confessed in a letter to Mme du Deffand on January 27, 1775, Trinity Great Court *was* the Castle of Otranto. Lastly, he was influenced by Gray, whose taste and medieval researches impressed him.

Walpole's improvements were made slowly because he was by no means so wealthy as to afford extravagant measures. The first transformation was not completed until 1753; and then sections went up from time to time to make an attractive but irregular structure, a happy blend of castellated and religious Gothic: the great parlor and library in 1754, the Holbein chamber or bedroom in 1759; the round tower, gallery, and the great cloister beneath it, and cabinet or little chapel in 1763; the great north bedchamber in 1772; the Beauclerc tower in 1776, the last main addition to the house; and the new offices in 1790, a large separate building (almost as large as the house itself) to the southwest of the round tower.[16] These are only a few among the many rooms—about thirty in two and a half stories, exclusive of those in the new offices. Inevitably, under the circumstances, Walpole did not impose fanciful Gothic details on a rigid Classical framework. Apparently, he did not start with an over-all plan in mind to which he undeviatingly adhered. Thus, Strawberry Hill turned out to be an informal product of accretion like its genuinely medieval antecedents, "standing alone among houses of the period in its picturesque asymmetrical composition."[17]

Of all the rooms, which incidentally were not particularly spacious, the gallery was the most magnificient—"Fifty-six feet long, seventeen feet high, thirteen wide, without the five recesses," and it was decorated flamboyantly. "The ceiling [of fan vaulting] is taken from one of the side aisles of Henry VII's Chapel [at Westminster]. . . . The great door is copied from the north door of St. Alban's. . . . The side with recesses . . . is taken from the tomb of Archbishop Bourchier at Canterbury." The walls were hung with crimson damask of Renaissance design, and the chairs and settees were similarly upholstered. Gray described this room as "all Gothicism and gold, and crimson, and looking glass,"—elements the revivalists combined without a twinge.[18] The net effect of this room can be visualized as having achieved the colorful and decorative intentions of rococo.

Indeed, Gray (writing to Wharton on September 18, 1754) admired "the spirit of Strawberry-Castle; it has a purity and propriety of Gothicism in it (with very few exceptions) which I have not seen elsewhere." Thus, as this praise suggests, it was really the archeological accuracy of the extensive artistic recreations of Gothic that made Strawberry Hill so original and so much admired in its time. Walpole had only contempt for the architects Batty Langley and Saunderson Miller, who he claimed simply had not understood the genuine article. According to him, Langley fatuously added Gothic trimmings to Classical forms, thereby producing a "bastard Gothic" (to Montagu, July 22, 1751). But at Strawberry Hill every detail was based on a medieval precedent, the real thing or an old print of it, though with no respect for the structural purpose of the original: a rose window in Old St. Paul's was the model for a ceiling; the chapter-house of York Minster became a small closet; medieval motifs of archiepiscopal and secular tombs at Westminster Abbey or at Canterbury decorated chimney pieces and even the piers of the garden gates; the library bookcases were modeled on a screen in Old St. Paul's; and the screen of the Abbot's Garden was taken from a bishop's tomb in Old St. Paul's; rich silk wallpaper painted in perspective to represent medieval fretwork, and lath and plaster made to resemble fan-vaulting were substituted for stone.

Strawberry Hill was the Gothic of an antiquary and man of taste, but the owner did not exclusively trust his own taste. He was ably assisted by an architect, his trusted friend, John Chute (1701–76) and a draughtsman, Richard Bentley (1708–82), the same artist (as indicated in the first chapter) who designed the decorations for Gray's *Odes*. These two gentlemen, together with himself, comprised the "Committee of Taste" responsible for the reconstruction. Walpole, the antiquary, provided the research utilized by the others in their designs. The builder responsible for the construction was William Robinson of the government's Board of Works. Undoubtedly, too, from time to time, Walpole must have had the advice of his good friends who visited Strawberry Hill at Christmas and Easter–George Selwyn, the wit; George James Williams, the connoisseur, and Richard Lord Edgecumbe, the comptroller of the royal household. Their portrait by Reynolds was hung over the chimney in the great parlor, or refectory.[19]

The total effect was that of a hybrid Gothic–a blend largely of two styles, the castellated (battlements, turrets, round tower) and religious (colored windows, pointed arches, vaulted-galleries, pinnacles, and decorations–rosettes, trefoil and quatrefoil forms and shields). It may be described as Gothic Rococo–a term that may help explain the character of the house and its decorative style to later generations. For it is true that although the stylistic imitations appeared to be authenticated, every original was effectively transformed by the "Committee of Taste" into something lighter and more elegant. They especially delighted in fretwork and filigree of any sort. Thus Strawberry Hill gave sophistication and fashionable grace to Gothic by lightening it with exuberant rococo detail. And this was not difficult to do, for it was the ornate and delicate late Perpendicular that was favored. Bristling pinnacles, elaborate ceilings, abundant windows are all characteristic of the flamboyant Perpendicular, late English Gothic style.

Walpole in letters, for instance, expressed his pleasure in "the great delicacy and richness" of Gothic ornaments, of "the florid Gothic."[20] As Clark observes, the neo-Gothic of Strawberry Hill has a certain gay exuberance remote from strict Gothic, especially Bentley's work on the fireplace and chimney in the great parlor, the yellow bedchamber, and the staircase. The fireplaces are embellished with pinnacles of the most attenuated kind; and the bookcases of the library are topped by flamboyant arches between pinnacles, while the ceiling is elaborately adorned with fretwork and medallions painted on a flat surface. Such exquisite elaboration, obviously, is a far cry from the stern massive forms of medieval castles.

This description of the hybrid, or eclectic, and rococo character of

Walpole's villa need not imply negative criticism. Walpole was not at all interested in completely authentic Gothic construction. For it was primarily the pictorial and romantic spirit of Gothic that he wished to capture—the "gloomth," "magic," and charm of the Gothic atmosphere, a combination of intimacy and fairyland, elegance and surprise.[21] Walpole himself thought of Strawberry Hill as a model antiquarian work which might inspire others to follow (to Mann, March 4, 1753). It was designed, he declared, to exhibit "specimens of Gothic architecture, as collected from standards in cathedrals and chapel tombs" and to show "how they may be applied to chimney pieces, ceilings, windows, balustrades, loggias, etc."[22]

He was fully aware, however, of Strawberry's qualities, defects, incongruities of modern and medieval decoration, its diminutive scale, and the insubstantial character of what he called "a paper fabric," a "fantastic fabric." It was, he said, "a small capricious house" in which he did not intend the decorations and furnishings to be strictly Gothic: "In truth, I did not mean to make my house so Gothic as to exclude convenience, and modern refinements in luxury. . . . It was built to please my own taste, and in some degree to realize my own visions." At the end of his life he admitted to Mary Berry (October 17, 1794) that "Every true Goth must perceive that they [the rooms at Strawberry Hill] are more the works of fancy than of imitation." Walpole obviously wished to avoid monkish gloom. He wanted to make the place habitable, comfortable, and cheerful. Indeed, even to this day, the interior suggests gaiety, including the chapel with all its gilt. The building has an unmistakable quality suggestive of frivolity, a frolicsome and playful attitude.

Although most of the details originally had somber religious associations, Walpole did not wish to think of Strawberry Hill as a religious monument. In his time, because of his collector's zeal, Strawberry Hill resembled a veritable museum and art gallery—the rooms were filled with a huge assortment of bric-a-brac illustrating those aspects of the past that intrigued Walpole and his fashionable contemporaries; and all the walls were hung with paintings, drawings, and prints. Even the imitation chapel ("The Tribune"), like the other major rooms, was used to display his collection of curiosities, antiques, artifacts, "objects of virtu"—cabinet pictures, miniatures, enamels, jewels, snuff-boxes, the hair of King Edward IV, the dagger of Henry VIII, a small bust in bronze of Caligula with silver seals, a silver bell by Benevenuto Cellini, and the like. The list of items in his *Description* is almost endless. Horace Walpole's was a thoroughly secular mind, although once he did express the fear that the gaudiness of this room was a little profane.[23]

The historical importance of Strawberry Hill, Walpole's country seat, rests upon the social prestige of its owner. Walpole stamped with the seal of fashionable approbation a style which had been regarded as a pleasing whimsicality on the level of rococo and chinoiserie. Certainly, he did not originate the taste for Gothic architecture or decoration; but with the success of his building—"The first English country house modelled upon an English country house, howbeit of an imaginary antique type, instead of classical buildings or practical convention"[24]—he did much to make it fashionable among the aristocratic *haut monde*. Strawberry Hill, being near London, was easily available; and Walpole was hospitable to visitors—indeed, proud to exhibit his miniature castle. His picturesque and rococo Gothic became truly fashionable, and it inspired later architects. Ultimately it spread round the globe, from Lee Priory and Fonthill to Government House at Sydney and the buildings on American campuses up to the last generation.

In the eighteenth century, Strawberry Hill became one of the most famous buildings in England, a showpiece and tourist attraction; and Walpole had tickets printed on his private press for visitors who wished to view the house and study its contents. The continuing glamor of Strawberry Hill meant a good deal to Walpole, and his ego was flattered by the attention it drew to him. Building it satisfied some deep inner need and, at the same time, gave him a focus of esthetic interest which endured to the end of his life.

Strawberry Hill is also of literary importance. For in remodeling his home in the country, Walpole provided substantial images that satisfied the craving of his imagination for the suggestive romantic "gloomth" and wildness of the Gothic style in architecture. His oft-quoted letter of March 9, 1765, to the antiquary William Cole, describes, for example, the genesis of his novel in a dream about a gigantic hand in armor on the uppermost bannister of a great staircase. In the last paragraph of the first Preface to *The Castle of Otranto,* he also says,

Though the machinery is invention, and the names of the characters imaginary, I cannot but believe that the ground-work of the story is founded on truth. The scene is undoubtedly laid in some real castle. The author seems frequently, without design, to describe particular parts. *The chamber,* says he, *on the right hand; the door on the left hand; the distance from the chapel to Conrad's apartment:* these and other passages are strong presumptions that the author had some certain building in his eye.

Thus it is true to say that in a large sense the Castle of Otranto, the vision or dream, was projected into the real life Strawberry Hill;[25] and, even further, that the gallery at Otranto was the real gallery at Strawberry Hill. The same could be said for many other rooms—the tribune, the blue bedchamber, the armory, as well as the staircase and the cloisters.[26] Of course, there are discrepancies between the two (Otranto was arranged around a courtyard, but Strawberry was not; Otranto had a great hall with an impressive staircase, a boarded gallery with latticed windows, and an oriel window, but Strawberry had merely a tiny stair-hall and no latticed gallery; Otranto had a small chamber on the stairs and a subterranean passage to a church, but Strawberry had neither);—discrepancies explained by his blending details taken from Trinity College, Cambridge, its courtyard, towers, gates, chapel, and hall, and details from other colleges of the university, with those of Strawberry Hill.[27] Yet despite these differences, which in no way weaken the intensity of the fundamental Gothic influence, Horace Walpole himself thought of Strawberry Hill as "a very proper habitation of, as it was the scene that inspired, the author of *The Castle of Otranto.*"[28] In the revival of Gothic architecture originated the Gothic novel.

III   *Art Historian and Critic:* Anecdotes of Painting

Walpole's capacity for sustained intellectual effort is demonstrated by his monumental *Anecdotes of Painting* (1762-71), a history of art in England, including painting (portraits, landscape, historical), architecture, sculpture, engraving, medals, enamels and miniatures, from the earliest times to the accession of George III.[29] "By this publication, Horace Walpole," declares Lionel Cust, "laid the foundations for an historical study of the Fine Arts in England, which to this day has proved the chief authority for reference upon this subject." Indeed, according to Cust, Walpole owes his immortality and literary fame not only to the letters but also to the authoritative *Anecdotes,* for in this history—his most ambitious work—he was a pioneer, and the work as a result of his painstaking care is still a standard source for the biographies of hundreds of artists, the most important basic source of information on art in England before 1750.[30]

"This country," Walpole wrote in the preface, explaining and justifying the history, "which does not always err in vaunting its own productions, has not a single volume to show on the works of its painters."[31] Admitting that England produced few good artists, he therefore felt he could not entitle it *The Lives of English Painters* in imitation of Giorgio Vasari's famous work. Instead, he used *Anecdotes of Painting in England*, choosing the word "anecdotes" because it reflects the basically informative purpose of the work. The word "anecdotes," according to the *Oxford English Dictionary*, meant in its early sense (literally from the Greek) "secret, or hitherto unpublished narratives or details of history."

Walpole had purchased an enormous collection of notes and writings on English art from the widow of the painter and friend of his father, George Vertue (1684–1756), who had thought of compiling a history from them. Some insight into the nature of his problem is given in a letter to Pinkerton on October 15, 1788: "Vertue's manuscripts are not only a heap of unmethodic confusion, but are written in so very diminutive a hand that, many years ago, when I collected my 'Anecdotes' from them, and had very strong eyes, I was often forced to use a magnifying glass." Although Walpole himself modestly admits only to performing an editorial job, his capacity for editing, even so, should not be minimized. For his is a truly masterly résumé of their contents—he rewrote every article, checked sources in books, organized the materials, added a good deal of information on his own, and, in short, presented the material in a polished, lively style which made it readable and comprehensible, always informative and, to his antiquarian friends, entertaining, and to us occasionally delightful. The essay on the dispersion of Charles I's collection, it may be said, possesses all these qualities.

When we look at the enormous mass of Vertue's scattered and inchoate memoranda in the seven Walpole Society volumes (1930–55), Walpole's achievement in digesting and rearranging them into the coherent and lucid literary form of the *Anecdotes* appears all the more remarkable. Nor is Walpole's work entirely unoriginal. Even before he had purchased Vertue's notebooks he had begun his history; and, besides, he had other sources of information in addition to Vertue's compilations. He had amassed a fund of knowledge of his own in the course of his own peregrinations round the country seats of England— he took notes on the art and architecture of forty-five such houses which he visited between 1751 and 1784.[32] He had studied the best collections of art at home and abroad. He had worked on many catalogues, beginning with the one on his father's immense collection at Houghton Hall. He himself had amassed the most complete collection of Hogarth prints in the century and had carefully catalogued Hogarth's works, as well as prints by other engravers; and again, according to his own account, he had a large collection of engravings by the early masters and, as noticed before, the best individual collection of printed heads, miniatures, and enamels in the country (III,462). Vertue's notes were thus only one of the sources of Walpole's information. If anything, the *Anecdotes* demonstrates Walpole's ability to observe comprehensively, to record carefully and faithfully, to comment shrewdly. The enormity, the sheer labor, of this exhaustive work cannot be associated with the character of a mere dilettante.

The *Anecdotes,* really the work of a learned scholar, suggests the stereotype of the studious antiquary as the master of minutiae. And Walpole thought of himself as an earnest antiquary, as a comment about Henry VIII's Reformation makes clear: "There is no forgiving him that destruction of ancient monuments and gothic piles and painted glass by the suppression of monasteries; a reformation, as he called it, which we antiquaries almost devoutly lament." Likewise he deplored the destructiveness of the Civil War—"An area we antiquaries lament with no less devotion than the former" (III, 52). In *A Catalogue of Engravers* he writes appreciatively yet humorously of other antiquaries like himself with whom he easily established rapport:

The writers of that age [the seventeenth century], though now neglected by their uncouth style, their witticisms, and want of shining abilities, are worth being consulted for many anecdotes and pictures of manners, which are to be found nowhere else. What variety of circumstances are preserved by Lloyd, Winstanley, and such obsolete biographers! Fuller, amidst his antiquated wit, yet wit it was, is full of curious, though perhaps minute information. His successor, Anthony Wood, who had no more notion of elegance than a scalping Indian, nor half so much dexterity in hacking his enemies, is inexhaustibly useful (IV, 34).

What he says about this *Catalogue* also applies to the *Anecdotes,* as he expresses the hope that collectors will thank him for his pains, "for, if the drudgery of collecting is dull, what is it to be a collector's collector!" (IV, 38)

His weariness caused by the long hours industriously spent at his writing occasionally had the effect of making him diffident about the meaning of his labors. But the compulsion of the antiquary—to hunt down the fact and to record it—prevailed. He felt that he had to do the job, to provide the catalogue, to honor the artist, to help fellow collectors, and to raise standards of taste among the innocent public.

Particularly, he owed collectors the facts. Writing about one engraver, he explains, " . . . as my author [Vertue] had formed a long list, it would be defrauding curious collectors if I refused to transcribe it: one would not grudge a few hours more, after the many that have been thrown away on these idle volumes. I seem to myself a door-keeper at the Temple of Fame, taking a catalogue of those who have only attempted to enter" (IV, 84). One of his affectations was to pretend not to be a scholar and to scoff at all who were. Such is his inherited aristocratic prejudice. But the *Anecdotes* must be considered as proof of the paradox that in England the amateur is often, by his own choice and endeavors, the scholar. Walpole is living evidence of that near-impossibility—the learned gentleman.

The *Anecdotes* is basically an archeological compendium, not a critical history of art. It contains very many "brief or trifling articles" on artists. As Walpole himself admits, "This work is but an essay towards the history of our arts; all kinds of notices are inserted, to lead to further discoveries." He intended the work "as an impartial register of, not as a panegyric on, our English artists." Yet this does not mean that he does not employ his critical faculty "in commending and blaming" (III, 316−17, 432). His essay on a contemporary, William Hogarth (including the comprehensive catalogue of Hogarth's prints), may be cited as an excellent illustration of his art criticism, judicious yet balanced by sympathetic warmth and appreciative understanding of Hogarth's artistic and moral aims. Walpole, always sensitive to the ability of the best artists to portray and evoke emotion, seizes on just this quality in Hogarth's "delicate and superior" comic satire— "familiarized by strokes of nature and heightened by wit, and the whole animated by proper and just expressions of the passions." But Walpole also believed that "as a painter he had but slender merit," thinking that that was not the real bent of Hogarth's genius. Nor was he impressed by Hogarth's so-called discovery of the principle of grace— the serpentine line of beauty.[33] There are, then, in the *Anecdotes* enough evidences to show Walpole in the capacity of serious art critic as well as art historian. From this point of view, his critical opinions are most interesting for our study and may contribute to an understanding not only of his taste but also of his personality.

Among his best essays are those dealing with architecture, and his remarks help explain the alterations at Strawberry Hill. He writes with verve when he focuses on architecture, especially his favored Gothic style.[34] His prose becomes animated, often crackling and sparkling with irony and epigrammatic wit, and he exhibits the confidence of an expert. "Beautiful Gothic architecture," he declares, "was engrafted on Saxon deformity," by which he meant Norman or Romanesque architecture. It is easy to see why, as noted in our discussion of Strawberry Hill, he was attracted to the Gothic; particularly the late Gothic, where detail ran riot: "The pointed arch, that peculiar of Gothic architecture, was certainly intended as an improvement on the circular; and the men who had not the happiness of lighting on the simplicity and proportion of the Greek orders, were, however, so lucky as to strike out a thousand graces and effects, which rendered their buildings magnificent, yet genteel, vast, yet light, venerable and picturesque." He is pleased by the appeal to the picturesque and to the romantic emotions and associations of ideas:

It is difficult for the noblest Grecian temple to convey half so many impressions to the mind, as a cathedral does of the best Gothic taste—a proof of skill in the architects and of address in the priests who erected them. The latter exhausted their knowledge of the passions in composing edifices whose pomp, mechanism, vaults, tombs, painted windows, gloom and perspectives infused such sensations of romantic devotion; and they were happy in finding artists capable of executing such machinery.

Then follows the oft-quoted epigram that sharply contrasts the rational Greek with the romantic Gothic: "One must have taste to be sensible of the beauties of Grecian architecture; one only wants passions to feel Gothic." The context (generally overlooked), an expression of distaste for popery and superstition, shows that Walpole cannot easily shed fundamentally conditioned attitudes, despite the fact that he is aware of Gothic appeal to agreeable romantic passions: "though stripped of its [Westminster Abbey] altars and shrines, it is nearer converting one to popery than all the regular pageantry of Roman domes. Gothic churches infuse superstition; Grecian admiration" (III, 93-94).

What he wished to capture with his adaptation of medieval Gothic at Strawberry Hill was, of course, its picturesque quality and its romantic associations—in accordance with the spirit of Gothic, as he describes it with equal vivacity in another part of the *Anecdotes:* "the bold scenery of Gothic architecture, with all its airy embroidery and pensile vaults" (III, 430). In the fragmentary fifth volume, these associations that affect the passions, he explains, account clearly for his medieval preferences:

I think the Gothic would strike most at first, the Grecian would please the longest. . . . I who have great difficulty of not connecting every inanimate thing with the idea of some person, or of not affixing some idea of imaginary persons to whatever I should see, should prefer that building that furnished me with most ideas, which is not judging fairly of the merit of the buildings abstractedly. And for this reason, I believe the gloom, ornaments, magic of the hardiness of the buildings, would please me more in the Gothic than the simplicity of the Grecian.[35]

Thus, because he favored the magically light and romantically suggestive touch—which he found in the late Perpendicular flamboyant style, "the richness and delicacy of the Gothic"—he disliked the "stately mansions" constructed in Elizabeth I's reign in "that bastard style which intervened between Gothic and Grecian architecture"; he disliked the crude and heavy work of Sir John Vanbrugh who "with his ponderous and unmeaning masses [at Blenheim and Castle Howard] overwhelmed architecture in mere masonry." He also rejected the work of James Gibbs, who, incidentally, had added the cupolas to the four corners of the central building at Houghton and built the Classically styled King's College where Walpole resided as a young man. He is unable to find any grace or ease or harmonious simplicity, nature or taste, in the work of Gibbs who like Vanbrugh was only capable of "gigantic and clumsy grandeur." King's College next to the admired chapel does appear, it is true, "only regularly heavy."[36]

On the other hand, he honored the Palladian "purity" of work of the Earl of Burlington, under whose patronage "architecture . . . recovered its genuine lustre"; and he had high praise for Burlington's disciple William Kent as "the father of modern gardening." However, Walpole thinks that Kent's work as painter was inferior, and as architect mediocre (III, 437, 486–88).

With regard to painting, that he recommended the English landscape as a suitable subject is noteworthy: "Our ever-verdant lawns, rich vales, fields of haycocks, and hop-grounds, are neglected as homely and familiar subjects. The latter which I never saw painted, are very picturesque. . . " (III, 450–51). Yet, despite this opinion, it is surprising to note his neglect of Richard Wilson; however, he does commend the "frankness of nature" in the landscapes of Thomas Gainsborough (III, 399).

In general, Walpole is an exciting critic, praised for his taste and competence by all who have written on the subject. He often writes with vigorous pungency—as of Piranesi who "has a sublime savageness in his engravings like Salvator Rosa." He takes his stand on fashions: William Chambers' *Treatise on Oriental Gardening* is "a work that tended to bring back all manner of bad and whimsical taste."[37] He writes zestfully and yet judiciously, with shrewdness and sensibility in his penetrating critiques of Hogarth as well as Reynolds. Praising and blaming these artists in detail, he demonstrates his shrewd insight and sensitive intelligence.[38] The essay on Hogarth is still considered a standard one on the subject. He errs only when he is concerned with the works of his close friends and social equals. Thus in his very last chapter of the supplementary fifth volume, he paid homage to those of his own circle, "Ladies and Gentlemen Distinguished by their Artistic Talents." He overpraises the house, grounds, and "offskip," or views, of his intimate Henry Seymour Conway; and the artistic powers of other close associates—Richard Lord Edgecumbe, Conway's daughter Mrs. Damer, and Lady Diana Beauclerc who "had an amazing genius for drawing, music, and all the arts, and the most exquisite taste."[39]

In fine, the *Anecdotes of Painting* show Walpole as the English Vasari, although he would modestly offer a disclaimer. That he was wholly serious about art is made abundantly clear in this massive and entirely conscientious work—the ultimate authority on art before 1750. His concern with the arts was not the frivolous pleasure of a dilettante, one who prefers what is amusing in art to anything else. That he was broad-minded in his opinions about art is also seen in his championing Gothic, and that he showed magnanimity, sensitivity and good sense is seen in his exact and objective appraisals, particularly the criticism of his contemporary William Hogarth.

IV   *Gardenist:* The History of Modern Gardening[40]

Among Horace Walpole's many interests was a lively one in landscape design. His wealth afforded him the opportunity to put some of his ideas into practice. His social position permitted him to spread his ideas effectively among those who could also afford to cultivate this fashionable but expensive hobby. Walpole spent a good deal of his time advising his wealthy friends who were landscaping their estates. He even wrote a formal treatise on the subject, which he appended to his voluminous *Anecdotes of Painting.*

To begin, Walpole's appreciation of nature, which is a significant part of his total esthetic position, is largely in the "picturesque" stage of observation; that is, he generally saw nature through the trained, sophisticated vision of one to whom the painted landscapes of Salvator Rosa, Claude Lorrain, and Gaspar and Nicholas Poussin, among others, were well known. Comparing scenery to pictures was habitual with him, thereby suggesting that the charms of recognition and learned picturesque allusion were of primary significance rather than the sensing of the divine presence.[41] The two arts of painting and landscaping were so closely linked in his mind that it was natural for him to include, as the final chapter of his history of painting, a history of English experiments in a new type of landscape design. His attitude remained at this level of interest to the end of his days; he was incapable, or if this is too severe a criticism, he did not think of responding to the deeper, spiritual and transcendental, naturalistic sublime. After returning from his Grand Tour when he crossed the Alps, he never (unlike Gray) visited places where he could again be excited by wild natural scenery—the Highlands of Scotland, the Lake District, or the Wye River Valley, or any part of Wales.

His well-known letter to Richard West about his visit with Gray to the Grande Chartreuse in the Savoy (September 28–30, 1739), even though written long before he thought of theoretical problems of landscape art and its relationship with nature, demonstrates that his picturesque attitude was formed at Houghton early in life. There his father's collection included paintings by Salvator Rosa and Gaspar Poussin.[42] In this letter, Walpole thinks first of Salvator; but Gray, in a letter on the same episode, thinks of the transcendental wild sublime, of religion and poetry. At the end of his letter, it is true, Walpole writes: "We . . . wished for a painter, wished to be poets"—but the context means descriptive painter-poets, of course. His attitude favoring the picturesque rather than the genuinely spiritual or romantic, Walpole felt that only landscape painters and scenic poets could faithfully describe this scenic beauty. It is thus no accident that the features of the landscape which excited him in the mountains of the Savoy coincided with many of the elements of the new picturesque garden he favored later in his life—the winding road, the hanging wood, the cascades, the old foot-bridge, the cottage, and the ruined hermitage.

Walpole's treatise, *The History of the Modern Taste in Gardening,* was written probably between 1750 and 1770, when he was most active in the planning of his country estate and when his interest in gardening was naturally most intense. This work provides additional evidence of the kind of person he was and the kind of taste he had, as do the architectural design and the collection of Strawberry Hill. It may also be regarded as one of the best contemporary histories of the change in attitude toward nature, especially toward landscape gardening, which took place in the mid-eighteenth century. The author's chief purpose is to promulgate the new naturalistic or irregular style in landscaping English parks and to oppose the neo-Classic symmetrical garden. The latter, the old-fashioned garden, was after the manner of André LeNôtre, who landscaped Versailles: a formal garden, with long, graveled walks and with trees and shrubbery clipped into fantastic shapes, with marble steps climbing into the air at the end of vistas, and basins into which water purled.

Generally, however, in his enthusiasm for nature and in his fully developed theory, Walpole cannot be considered a deeply committed Romantic. Conscious strategy was too much a part of his attitude. He felt that a conscious, but concealed, art must be added to the bare imitation of nature in order to create beauty, and that a technique of landscape design similar to the technique of painting was necessary to create gardens which follow the principles of the picturesque. True, his basic assumptions may be considered Romantic—that untouched nature is inherently good and beautiful; hence that natural variety and irregularity should be the bases of all gardening. According to this reasoning, formal gardens in the architectural style are simply evidences of false taste, ostentation, and love of luxury. But Walpole himself did not care to leave nature alone. He advocated that she be touched up, if only discreetly, for deliberate picturesque effect.

Walpole was original in his analysis of the "sunk fence," fosse or haha! as the "capital stroke" which brought about the new English garden. This subtly concealed ditch, he said, was originally Charles Bridgman's innovation, but William Kent developed its potential: "He leaped the fence and saw that all nature was a garden. He felt the delicious contrast of hill and valley changing imperceptibly into each other, tasted the beauty of the gentle swell, or concave scoop, and remarked how loose groves crowned an easy eminence with happy ornament, and while they called in the distant view between their graceful stems, removed and extended the perspective by delusive comparison."

In the old formal garden, each part surrounded by a boundary was considered a distinct unit; each was unrelated to the others except by connecting paths; and, within each unit, the treatment might vary tremendously. But according to the modern esthetics, when the entire property was "included in a kind of general design," each part necessarily became subordinate to the unity of the whole; each part had to be planted in harmony with the general scheme: "When nature was taken into the plan . . . every step that was made pointed out new beauties and inspired new ideas." It was this conception that became the basis of his complete naturalistic theory.

And such was the new garden, or English park, that he advocated.

Indeed, when we begin to visualize it, we find that it is not very much different from the primitivist view of simplicity propagated by Alexander Pope in his well-known moral satire, "The Epistle to Burlington (1731): "In all, let Nature never be forgot,/But treat the Goddess like a modest fair. . . . " "The living landscape," Walpole declares, "was chastened or polished, not transformed." "The gentle stream was taught to serpentize seemingly at its pleasure"; it should display neither the tortuous windings of the wild reformers nor the straight lines of the sixteenth-century canal. The natural forms of trees and shrubs should be allowed freedom to develop. Topiary work was taboo, as well as "clipt hedges, avenues, regular platforms, straight canals."[43] Buildings should be kept subordinate to the landscape. Most important, art or design must always be concealed, and the "genius," or character, of a landscape must be preserved, whatever its irregularity, variety, intricacy, or surprise. To Walpole, "the spirit of the landscape" came to have a definite organic individuality, which contained within itself the elements of irregular design, and which must in no way be violated.

Walpole singled out William Kent, painter and landscapist, for successfully "improving nature" and for realizing the ideals of the English garden. To him, Kent was "the father of modern gardening"; "the inventor of an art that realizes painting and improves nature."[44] As we should expect, it is especially the capacity to see with a painter's eye that Walpole finds important in Kent's work. Kent's skill in painting had given him unusual insight into the possibilities of natural landscape. Kent was "painter enough to taste the charms of landscape" and to see what changes followed upon the removal of walls and hedges: "Thus the pencil of his imagination bestowed all the arts of landscape on the scenes he handled. The great principles on which he worked were perspective, and light and shade." Depth and breadth, the perspective in landscape painting, take the place of the linear architectural effects of the neo-Classic garden. Kent "realized the composition of the greatest masters in painting." Thus Walpole saw painting and gardening as but two different aspects of the same art—indicating clearly his view of nature as "picturesque gardening." His definition of this new garden style, perhaps anticipating William Gilpin's, appears not in the *History of Modern Gardening* but in the *Anecdotes of Painting: "the art of creating landscape"* by laying out ground "on principles of natural picturesque beauty, in contradistinction to symmetrical gardens."[45]

At Strawberry Hill, Walpole's own landscape garden of fourteen acres (tiny in comparison with huge parks like Stourhead) was informal and planned in the new manner, like that of Pope's Villa at nearby Twickenham. Walpole's garden, designed to contrast with the solemnity of the Gothic house, was supposed to provide a gay variety of scene. It had the typical sunken fence or haha which achieved a long unbroken vista. A long serpentine walk around the periphery of the grounds provided intricacy and surprise at the same time that it gave the illusion of size. Walpole subtly planned a succession of pictures along this walk which led one from a contemplation of the surrounding country and the busy life of the river Thames into the peace and quiet of cool, dark woods. Around each bend, Walpole placed some feature of interest to please the imagination with its unexpectedness, such as a Gothic chapel, a large antique Roman sarcophagus in marble, statues of Apollo and Daphne in bronze, a sleeping Morpheus "in plaster," and a shell bench carved in oak at the end of the winding walk. Groups of trees were planted naturally in the meadow to form a gradual link between the house and the wooded and wilder portions of the property (to Mann, June 12, 1753). A natural meandering stream cut across the property, feeding a round pool (in which Walpole bred goldfish) and eventually joining the Thames. This stream was spanned by a couple of Gothic bridges. In sum, then, this garden had the characteristics of intricacy and irregularity which excited surprise and a variety of emotions.

Yet, despite its diversity, it also had unity of design. The cloisters faced a stretch of lawn, at the end of which was the famous view of the Thames and Richmond Hill. This was the focal point toward which the planting opened—and the landscape was designed to lead toward it rather than to present rival points of interest. Such was the beautiful prospect that Walpole enjoyed from his windows or his garden—a natural and appropriate and designed feature, a unified "picturesque" composition of an English landscape.[46]

Horace Walpole's views on naturalistic gardening represent those of the eighteenth-century elite, the men of leisure and fashionable taste. Broadly speaking, like his interest in Gothic architecture and romance, his innovations in garden design contributed to the trend in art which favored a freer and more naturalistic style; and for this reason his theory and practice are important in the history of Romanticism. But we detect a certain fastidious and effeminate fussiness in his attitude toward nature, that of one who observes nature with the eye of a landscape painter. He desired nature to be gracefully elegant. Really, then, the fact that he felt gardens should resemble nature is not quite so significant as a norm for measuring his personality and the depth of his commitment to a genuinely Romantic point of view as that he insisted that all nature ought to resemble a garden, or a painted landscape. Like other evidences of his taste, Walpole's interest in landscape gardening reflects his leisure-class bias; his romantic naturalism is typically aristocratic.

CHAPTER 4

The Storyteller

I *A Gothic Dream:* The Castle of Otranto

ACCORDING TO his preface to the first edition, Walpole thought that in *The Castle of Otranto* he was presenting his readers with an historical novel.[1] Thus from his point of view, he tried faithfully to depict the customs of the Middle Ages, and his narrative may be considered as a product of his antiquarian research. But, lacking confidence in his abilities, and uncertain of this novel's reception because of its novelty, Walpole disguised his authorship by declaring that the story was a translation by William Marshall of a work originally written in Italian by Onuphrio Muralto, canon of the Church of St. Nicholas in Otranto, that it was first printed in Naples in 1529, and that the action presumably occurred around the time of the Crusades between 1095 and 1243.

"The principal incidents," he writes, "are such as were believed in the darkest ages of Christianity"(3).[2] He imagines that "an artful priest" might have used his creative talent in the Counter Reformation against the rational Protestant reformers and innovators "to confirm the populace in their ancient errors and superstitions. . . . Such a work as the following would enslave a hundred vulgar minds beyond half the books of controversy that have been written from the days of Luther to the present hour" (3). What he has in mind are specifically "miracles, visions, necromancy, dreams, and other preternatural events" (4). His use of the supernatural rests upon the historical point of view.

Thus, almost with the zeal of an antiquary, Walpole projected his imagination into the medieval past. Like Bishop Richard Hurd who in his *Letters on Chivalry and Romance,* published two years before Walpole's tale, pleaded that Edmund Spenser's *Faerie Queene* should be read and criticized as a Gothic, not a Classical, poem, so Walpole wished to be "faithful to the *manners* of the times." As he wrote to his friend

Cole (March 9, 1765), "If I have amused you by retracing with any fidelity the manners of ancient days, I am content." Significantly, also, he changed the subtitle of the first edition from *A Story* to *A Gothic Story,* for he meant to classify his novel as a medieval narrative. All of those remarks indicate that in order to effect "this *air* of the *miraculous"* and to provide a coherent, consistent, and accurate picture of the Middle Ages, Walpole had to show the culture riddled by superstition. Yet, sensitive to any imputation of regressive religious irrationalism or enthusiam, he warned his readers to separate the artist from his work: "He is not bound to believe them himself ['every kind of prodigy'], but he must represent his actors as believing them" (4). At the same time that he justified his own practice through the historical point of view, it should be noted that he also expressed his usual antipathy to the primitive beliefs associated with the Roman Catholic Church.

In the work itself, however, imaginative sympathy with the supernatural, or historical imagination, is far more impressive than critical rationalism, or possible satire of medieval belief. Besides, in a novel of this sort, with emphasis on the pleasure taken in the sensations of terror, the satire would have been anachronistic and the hostile tone esthetically indefensible. Certainly, *The Castle of Otranto* is not read as a controversial tract that exposes and ridicules medieval Catholic superstition. But obviously such elements of naive belief are deliberately included in the work and are, at least with respect to Walpole's strong anti-Catholic bias, of some significance to an understanding of "the author's motives" (4) in writing this romance. Because they are the very first ideas that he discusses in the preface, they must have been important to him.

As for the other aspects of the art, Walpole, writing in the first preface according to the neo-Classical formulations of the Aristotelian poetic, insists that "the rules of drama are almost observed" (4) throughout the work: "It is pity that he [the author, Walpole himself] did not apply his talents to what they were evidently proper for, the theatre." Each chapter, and there are five to suggest a five-act tragedy, concludes with an exciting curtain that maintains suspense until the final exciting catastrophic climax, the destruction of the castle. Such suspense, too, is enhanced by terrifying sound effects—whistling winds, deep and hollow groans, creaking doors, mysterious rustling, thunder, or even absolute silence, as well as by half-finished sentences.

Walpole insists that there are no flowery figures of speech, "no digressions or unnecessary descriptions" to retard the action and relax the imagination. The novel, it is true, does illustrate a strict unity of action. This fact an outline of the plot substantiates: The only son of the villain Prince Manfred is discovered on the morning of his wedding crushed in the castle courtyard beneath an enormous helmet. Determined that his line shall not become extinct and the property inherited by some other family, Manfred decides to divorce his sterile wife Hippolita and to marry Isabella, his son's destined bride, daughter of Marquis Frederic of Vicenza who is reported dead. To escape from her pursuer, Isabella takes flight down a subterranean passage, where she is assisted by a "peasant" Theodore, who bears a curious resemblance to a portrait of the usurped Alfonso in the castle gallery.

At intervals the servants of the castle are alarmed by the sudden appearance of massive pieces of armor in different parts of the building. A clap of thunder shakes the castle to its foundations and heralds the culmination of the story. The apparition of the good Alfonso appears "dilated to an immense magnitude," collapsing the walls of the castle, and demands that Manfred shall surrender Otranto to the rightful heir, Theodore. His ghost pacified after the destruction of the castle, the figure of Alfonso ascends to heaven. Thereupon Father Jerome, completing Theodore's history, explains the circumstances of his birth and his relationship to Alfonso, and so the prophecy which opens the story ("That the castle and lordship of Otranto should pass from the present family, whenever the real owner should be grown too large to inhabit it.") is fulfilled at the end. Because Matilda, beloved of Theodore, has been accidentally slain by her father, the hero consoles himself with Isabella. Manfred abdicates, and he and his wife Hippolita retire to neighboring convents.

As for the other two dramatic unities, Walpole is also very much aware of them. The time of the action is limited to three days and two nights; the place, to the castle and its environs. Furthermore, the characters are sharply drawn and, Walpole insists, made to behave consistently in terms of probability, their type and plot function—even the low characters who are considered objects of humor. But we may well question whether all the characters are governed by the rule of probability. Obviously, the apparition of Don Alfonso is not. But, in defense, Alfonso—or the several parts of his corpse that appear from time to time—is responsible for most of the miracles at the core of the medieval superstition that Walpole wishes to represent.

However, what is more to the point, Manfred's accidental murder of his daughter Matilda is not well motivated. It is not enough to say that Manfred, blinded by drink and enraged by the belief that he overhears

Isabella and Theodore planning to thwart his cherished plan, acts with excessive haste. This important climactic episode is not carried through with conviction, for Manfred could just as well have stabbed Theodore, his antagonist, and thereby could have assured his possession of the girl. The inevitability of Manfred's behavior is clearly open to question, suggesting that he, like the others is a plot-ridden character, an oversentimentalized and melodramatic stereotype.

Merely to list the cast of characters is to demonstrate how cliché-ridden the novel is. These are stock characters: Manfred, the satanic, wicked and lustful prince with a "severe temper," haunted by the guilt of a secret crime committed long ago by his grandfather, the original usurper of Otranto; his pious and long suffering wife, saintly Hippolita; his lovely daughter, modest dutiful Matilda; a damsel in distress, the beautiful and helpless Lady Isabella, mistreated by wicked guardians and pursued by the tyrant; her father Frederic, who returns from the Holy Land to rescue her. Moreover, we also meet a hero, Theodore, who appears as a "mysterious stranger," a handsome, intelligent, and acutely sensitive young peasant who turns out to have true nobility of character—a birthmark identifies him as the rightful prince and heir and enables him to marry the virtuous princess Isabella; Theodore's father, the devout priest Jerome, formerly the Count of Falconara, who for consolation turns to the church and good works upon the loss of his wife and child;[3] three apparitions (of good Alfonso and wicked Ricardo, grandparents of the principals, and of the old hermit of the Holy Land, whose praying skeleton wrapped in a cowl reminds Frederic of his moral goal when he lusts for Matilda). In addition, as we have already mentioned, there are some silly servants, the chattering Bianca and Manfred's cowardly and moronic retainers, who serve to provide some comedy to soften the rigorously tragic tone.

Moreover, regarding the Classical rules of art which Walpole adopted, and each of which he discusses in the preface, the Aristotelian catharsis is used to justify this romance: terror and pity, the tragic passions, are evoked and purged, thereby sustaining the somber tone and effecting the full purpose of tragedy. Terror, Walpole writes, keeps up the excitement; and pity is introduced for contrast—or for sheer sentiment.[4] Indeed, Walpole is thoroughly neo-Classical in his approach to the art of this "drama," assuming that its beauties are inherent in the craft rules that he has deliberately observed. Even his introduction of the moral—the sins of ambition being visited on the children to the third and fourth generation—suggests his neo-Classical bias. According to him, this tale instructs and entertains; therefore it is exempt "from the censure to which romances are but too liable" (5).

Thus Walpole, reflecting uncertainty, propitiates the critics as he explains his craftsmanship in terms of all the old Classical rules and attempts to dignify his Romantic Gothicism by placing it squarely in the conservative critical tradition. *The Castle of Otranto* demonstrates far more conscious art than Walpole, in his letters describing his conception and composition of the novel, is willing to admit. But his justification of his Romantic tale by means of the Classical rules of tragic drama is a curious inversion of Bishop Hurd's historical method or of Walpole's own initial statement that a Gothic tale ought to be read and judged as a Gothic work. Many of his critical remarks on the novel may be considered as evidences of critical timidity and conservatism, of an aesthetic theory lagging far behind the demands of his imagination and taste preferences.

Certainly, too, with regard to Walpole's conscious art, the style lacks spontaneity. Turning to any page at random will exhibit the frigid elegance of a period piece. For example, when Manfred sees the portrait of his grandfather descend from its frame, he cries out: "Do I dream? or are the devils themselves in league against me? Speak, infernal spectre! Or, if thou art my grandsire, why dost thou too conspire against my wretched descendant. . . . Lead on! . . . I will follow thee to the end of perdition" (21).

And we have the following evidence of quaint prose and morality from Isabella, when Theodore invites the persecuted maiden to move deeper into the safety of a cave: "Alas! what mean you, sir? said she. Though all your actions are noble, though your sentiments speak the purity of your soul, is it fitting that I should accompany you alone into these perplexed retreats? Should we be found together, what would a censorious world think of my conduct?—I respect your virtuous delicacy, said Theodore; nor do you harbour a suspicion that wounds my honour" (60).

Nothing could be further from the refreshing and realistic colloquialism of Henry Fielding. True, this elegance has been praised by Walter Scott as "pure and correct English." But we cannot be impressed with such "chastity and precision of style"; we sense only an exquisite melodramatic sensibility intensified by a frosting of glittering artificiality.[5] Thus, because of this old-fashioned Romantic style, among all its other artistic properties, we cannot help thinking of *The Castle of Otranto* as a strange historical curiosity, and wishing, instead, for a taste of the delightfully vivid and often racy colloquialism of Walpole's letters.

Walpole's antiquarian learning is not only reflected in the self-conscious treatment of medieval Catholicism in Italy, but also in the details concerning medieval architecture and chivalry, armor and pageantry. As for the setting, it is surprising to see that although the assembling of properties is lavish, they are (just as Walpole indicates in his preface) unobtrusively and naturally presented. Walpole never formally describes the setting by itself; unlike Ann Radcliffe, he never paints a complete landscape in words. On the contrary, he always cites places or gives directions briefly whenever he must, in accordance with the demands of the swift action as the characters move about.

With regard to the castle itself, which is at the center of the romance, and which is created in scattered references, Walpole mentions (but does not describe) the following exterior props: "a brazen trumpet which hung without the gate of the castle," the gates in front and the postern gate in the rear as well as a bell at the back gate; the castle courtyard where the gigantic helmet falls and crushes young Conrad; the ramparts where Matilda and her mother once take the refreshing evening air after the feast. Interior details are mentioned in the same manner: the great hall where the banquet is held, and where Manfred questions Theodore and speaks to the Herald of the Knight of the Gigantic Sabre; at its upper end a boarded gallery with latticed windows through which Matilda sees Theodore and notes his resemblance to Alfonso as he is being questioned and threatened with execution by her father. The great hall also has an oriel window, in the recess of which Manfred tries to extract information from Bianca, Matilda's handmaid.

Off the great hall is an inner council chamber where Manfred privately interviews the visiting knights. Then, near the top of the great stairs, there are the great or gallery chamber or gallery with the portrait of Manfred's grandfather Ricardo, a door at one end, and another portrait of the usurped Alfonso the Good before which Maltida often prays; and, in addition, there are several chambers or private apartments for Maltida, Hippolita, and Manfred. There is also a chamber haunted by the ghost of the drowned tutor of young Conrad—the only haunted room in the castle. Next to Hippolita's chamber is her oratory, where Frederic, marquis of Vicenza (alias the Knight of the Gigantic Sabre), sees the praying skeleton of the hermit of Joppa that he had met in the Holy Land. There are many other rooms: a small chamber off the principal staircase where Theodore is kept for some time (probably the

haunted chamber); Matilda's apartment directly over it (thus the two
are permitted to converse through the opened windows of the
casements without seeing each other); Isabella's, which is "the
watchet-coloured [pale blue] chamber, on the right hand, one pair of
stairs" (81); and the chamber of Frederic, the visiting knight. The castle
also possesses an armory, from which Theodore borrows a full suit of
armor—and, after investing himself in armor, he bears a striking
resemblance to Alfonso, as Matilda notices again. Nor can we forget the
uppermost bannister of the great stairs, where the sight of the gigantic
ghostly hand in armor makes Bianca hysterical.

But Walpole does not stop here, for beneath the castle he points to
many more interesting architectural features. The lower part of the
castle is "hollowed into several intricate cloisters" and vaults, whose
silence is broken by the creak of rusty hinges as an occasional blast of
air sets an old door moving. There, a trapdoor with a trick lockspring
opens down to steps leading to a dark and secret subterranean passage
(a "labyrinth of darkness") to the Church of St. Nicholas nearby. This
is the most alarming feature of this sinister building. Poor Isabella,
pursued by the wicked Manfred, is terrified when the wind extinguishes
her lamp; but eventually, despite the handicap of darkness, she makes
her escape via this underground route to sanctuary with Father Jerome
in the church. There the black marble statue of Alfonso the Good and
his tomb in the chapel may be seen. Next to the church is the convent
or monastery which has been founded by Hippolita. Adjacent to the
castle, probably opposite to the church, is a "hospital" for pilgrims,
where the men of the knight's train are lodged. The town is on the west
side, and a forest and rocky caverns ("a labyrinth of caverns")
extending to the seacoast are to the east of the castle. At the mouth of
one of these caves "haunted by evil spirits," Theodore again discovers
Isabella, just as formerly he had found her in the dark vaults below the
castle, and here he wounds her father Frederic in combat.

As explained in the section on Walpole's villa, the castle is generally
Strawberry Hill enlarged, glorified, and enchanted, with some details
added from the Great Court of Trinity College and King's College
Chapel, Cambridge. As for Otranto itself, what Walpole told John
Pinkerton explains how he chose the name of the place in Apulia, in the
southeastern part of the old Kingdom of Naples: "Lady Craven has just
brought me from Italy a most acceptable present, a drawing of the
castle of Otranto. Here it is. It is odd that that back-window
corresponds with the description in my romance. When I wrote it, I did
not even know that there was a castle at Otranto. I wanted a name of

some place in the south of Italy, and Otranto struck me in the map.''[6]

Admittedly, this information about the castle is unsophisticated and nontechnical. Walpole is interested not so much in antiquarian or archeological accuracy as in enchanting atmospheric suggestiveness. He wished to produce a strange and terrifying effect, like that described in the opening lines of *The Mysterious Mother:*

> What awful silence! How these antique towers
> And vacant courts chill the suspended soul,
> Till expectation wears the cast of fear;
> And fear, half ready to become devotion,
> Mumbles a kind of mental orison,
> It knows not wherefore. . . .

Here in this vision of the haunted castle the whole of Gothic horror is neatly condensed; at the same time, superstition is provided with an appropriate sensational setting. So an "awful silence" reigns in the subterranean regions of the Otranto castle; and Manfred steals forward, "Gliding softly between the aisles, and guided by an imperfect gleam of moonshine that shone faintly through the illuminated windows."

That Walpole was esthetically correct in his strategy is our conclusion when we note with surprise how often his haunting images appeal to the visual sense and through it stimulate the imagination. Some of the supernatural Gothic effects are also produced somewhat casually as Walpole in the manner of vivid foreshortening and condensation of dream visions mentions the crashing fall of the monstrous helmet or casque with waving sable plumes that kills Conrad, or notes the sudden appearance of the gigantic armored hand, leg, and foot, and the other portions of the body scattered around the haunted castle.

However, in the treatment of medieval chivalry, particularly the elaborate description of the splendid procession of knights and warriors, he is somewhat less successful. But this is the only time that Walpole allows his antiquarian compulsion the freedom to describe "with . . . fidelity the manners of ancient days" (to Cole, March 9, 1765), and thereby to stop the forward action of the narrative. According to his account, the herald of the Knight of the Gigantic Sabre appears first, and this gentleman casts down his warder after challenging the usurper. Then the enormous train of the knight moves into the castle court—harbingers with wands, pages and trumpeters, footguards and horse, a hundred gentlemen bearing a huge sword, footmen in scarlet and black, a banner with the arms of Vicenza and

Otranto quarterly, the knight's confessor, two knights in complete armor with beavers down, squires with shields and devices, the principal knight in complete armor with lance at rest and face concealed by his vizor, closing with drums and trumpets—about 365 men all told! The fact that Walpole lingers over the colorful pageantry of this spectacular procession suggests enchantment, the hypnotic wonder of ritualistic dream; and certainly it contributes to what he has called "this *air* of the *miraculous.*" Considered rationally and functionally, however, it is obviously an overdone set piece which can only cause laughter.

The first edition proving successful, Walpole prepared another preface for the second edition in which he was unashamed to acknowledge his authorship of the novel. In this preface, he again explains his motives, "the grounds on which he composed it" (7). But this time he excludes remarks on his religious bias and focuses on his artistic purpose and his theory of narrative fiction, particularly that of the sensationalist Gothic novel. He sees *The Castle of Otranto* as "an attempt to blend the two kinds of romance, the ancient and the modern. In the former all was imagination and improbability: in the latter, nature is always intended to be, and sometimes has been, copied with success" (7). In the latter, which is, we presume, the realistic novel of manners developed by Samuel Richardson and Henry Fielding, "the great resources of fancy have been dammed up, by a strict adherence to common life." In the former, the old heroic romances, nature is "totally excluded."

Walpole wishes "to reconcile the two kinds"—to give fancy freedom by creating extraordinary situations and "to conduct the mortal agents in his drama according to the rules of probability" (8).[7] No doubt, it was his historical sense, as he explained in the first preface, that made possible this union of modern realism, everyday domestic life, or nature, and the Gothic imagination; for, as he indicated, belief in supernatural miracles prevailed in the Middle Ages to an extent that made any description of the life of those days inconceivable without them.

Soon, when a French translation of his romance appeared, Walpole in the oft-quoted letter to Mme du Deffand of March 13, 1767, avowed that of all his literary progeny *The Castle of Otranto* was his favorite child. In this letter he makes a plea for imagination and fantasy:

Let the critics have their say: I shall not be vexed: it was not written for this age, which wants nothing but cold reason. I own to you, and you will think me madder than ever, that of all my works, it is the only one in which I pleased myself: I let my imagination run: my visions and my passions kindled me. I wrote it in defiance of rules, critics, and philosophers [How untrue with respect to his own comments in the prefaces is most of this clause!], and it seems to me all the better for that. I am even convinced that in some later time when taste resumes the throne from which philosophy has pushed it, that my poor castle will find admirers; it has them even to-day coming on; I have just published the third edition.[8]

Supernatural evidences do not, of course, conform to the rules of probability. These, no doubt, Walpole had in mind in this letter as he preaches against rational philosophy or science and insists upon the validity of pure fantasy, expressed by oversized armor and weapons and several disembodied spirits, not to mention the evocation of terror by haunting groans and sighs coming from nowhere, sudden thunder and lightning, and the eerie darkness of the mysterious vaults and secret passages beneath the castle or in the gloomy caves among the rocks in the neighborhood.

All these creepy Gothic elements in *The Castle of Otranto* made it the novel that spawned the school of terror fiction. Walpole's words in the preface to the second edition were prophetic: he did strike out a "new route" that "paved a road for men of brighter talents" (8). Many of these innovations are absurd on the representational level of realism or what Walpole calls familiar or common nature; but they do suggest nightmare visions, and when added to the archetypal quality of the plot-ridden characters, the novel assumes the surrealist air of a bad dream.

In conclusion, we may very well ask, in the age of Freud, how this dream work reflects Walpole's own life. A clue is given in his letter to Cole, March 9, 1765. For, as a matter of fact, *The Castle of Otranto* originated in a dream, as Walpole himself explained in this letter. In the beginning of June, 1764, he had dreamt, he wrote to Cole, "that I thought myself in an ancient castle (a very natural dream for a head filled like mine with Gothic story) and that on the uppermost bannister of a great staircase I saw a gigantic hand in armour. In the evening I sat down and began to write, without knowing in the very least what I intended to say or relate." He worked at it with such intensity that he was able to complete it "in less than two months."[9]

He was "so engrossed" with this fantasy because, as he significantly admits, "I was very glad to think of anything rather than politics." Thus "the wildness of the story" may simply be a subliminal or stress reaction to some extremely irritating political events that had occurred in the days immediately preceding the dream. The facts concerning his tension and anxiety during these deeply disturbing days Walpole provides in his *Memoirs of George III*, particularly those memoranda in which he details his concern for his closest friend, Henry Conway, who in April, 1764, had been cut off by the king from his two sources of income as Groom of the Bedchamber and as commander of a regiment of dragoons for voting against the court on the issue of John Wilkes and General Warrants.

On the manifest level, then, the imaginary plot is united by a common theme of terrifying violence and conflict centered around the defeat of a tyrant. The surface incidents that detail the fall of this tyrant may express Walpole's current ambition in the spring and summer of 1764 to attain his father's power and to protect Conway. The tyrant Manfred represents the governmental power, king or court. Walpole himself can be identified first with the helpless son, Conrad, crushed and annihilated, and then with Theodore, the triumphant hero. Theodore overcomes all dangers and protects the virtuous and persecuted maiden, Isabella or Conway (in Walpole's relationship with him, Conway, Walpole's first cousin on his mother's side, always appears as a weak and indecisive creature of sterling virtue for whom Walpole had a good deal of affection)[10] and finally achieves the position held by his father. Even the title of Conway's position at court, Groom of the Bedchamber, can be brought into this first level interpretation to help establish his part in the Gothic tale of chambers, castles, chapels, underground passages, and mysterious portents. This surface meaning represents the current wish and anxiety for Conway's welfare that triggered the dream.

Going below the manifest level into the depths of the unconscious, we must be guided by Freud's Oedipal dream theories. There, in the unconscious, we learn that the manifest version represents the transvaluation of repressed dream thoughts and wishes; that is, these symbolic subterfuges and repressions, which are used to evade psychic censorship, are simply the distorted substitutes for the coherent organization of surface details. Assuming that these deeply repressed desires are Oedipal in character, we suggest that the following interpretation of the tale's very first paragraph is a possibility on this latent level of the prehistoric unconscious. The first sentence sets up the dual role for Walpole as both Matilda and Conrad, which the next sentence elaborates. The reference to "sickly" Conrad echoes the remark made by the seventy-year-old man who remembered what he had heard people whisper about himself when a child.[11] It suggests the author's own ineffectual nature, his inability to challenge his father.

The other portion of the sentence contains evidence of Walpole's typically ambivalent attitude toward his father. Thus, by projecting his split ego into two different people, Walpole's unconscious self expressed contradictory attitudes of tenderness and hostility. Moreover, by simple inversion Walpole's own ambivalence could be transferred to Manfred, who loved one child and disliked the other. Manfred, then, may represent Walpole's father, Sir Robert, who instills great respect and fear. Hippolita's motherly concern for Conrad may represent Lady Walpole's maternal and protective care of her sickly son. The reproaches of Manfred to Hippolita for her sterility suggest the unhappy marriage of Walpole's parents; Manfred's desire, upon Conrad's death, to divorce his wife and consummate a union with Isabella may also reflect Sir Robert's affair with Maria Skerritt, whom he married upon Lady Walpole's death.

The latent Oedipal themes, incest and mutilation, deriving from the infantile fear of punishment for the sin of incest, are suggested by the notion of sterility. Should we assume on the basis of dream condensation and distortion that Lady Isabella represents Lady Walpole, then what is revealed is Walpole's deeply unconscious and infantile desire for a sensual relationship with his mother. Finally, the prophecy which Manfred "dreads" (note the taboo implication) and which the peasants connect with the marriage, suggests the real meaning, that this is illicit passion. The ancient prediction simply discloses the child's secret ambition to grow up and assume the rights and duties of the father in an adult world. Ultimately, one central wish is exposed on this latent level, the infantile death wish for the father. Thus with the discovery of this crucial wish, even symbolized by inversion in the murder of Matilda at the end, the latent prehistoric theme of the dream is patricide, in association with the theme of incest.

In the resolution of the dream, Theodore is acknowledged as the "true Prince of Otranto"; he discovers a father in the good priest Jerome, and thereby expresses a wish-fulfillment of the youthful fancy for a kind, gentle, and virtuous father; and he also accepts the love of Isabella because "he could find no happiness, but in the society of one with whom he could forever indulge the melancholy that had taken possession of his soul" (90). The triumphant young hero has thus achieved the power of the father and acquired possession of the castle (a maternal symbol) and the undivided affection of the mother figure. Having wrested the dagger from Manfred and thereby rendered the tyrannical father impotent, Theodore relegates Manfred quite properly to a religious convent where he must remain as an emasculated celibate.

To conclude, then, the Oedipal situation, Freud's version of the family romance, has in some strangely familiar fashion structured Walpole's *Castle of Otranto.*

Here we can only suggest the possibility of such an analytic interpretation. Nor should we overlook the several erotic archetypal symbols—the ancient castle and its many chambers, the great staircase, the gigantic hand, immense foot and huge form of Alfonso, his enormous plumed helmet and his unwieldy sword, the underground passages, a locked door, forests, and caves—all of which also express latent thoughts, the psychic remnants of daily experience. So, all in all, this analysis demonstrates that the novel is not merely a consciously controlled literary phenomenon which Walpole in his two prefaces tries to explain and defend by means of a pathetically inadequate Classical formula. Nor is it only a curious museum exhibit which today can only be appreciated by a tortuous exercise of the historical imagination. But quite properly it is a dream work, a psychological fantasy possessing a uniquely personal meaning with universal implications. John Pinkerton records the following remark made by Walpole in 1784: "I am firmly convinced that a story might be written of which all the incidents should appear supernatural, yet turn out natural."[1 2] In the history of the Gothic novel this idea was developed by Ann Radcliffe, among Walpole's followers. Psychoanalysis, on the other hand, permits us to give rational and "natural" meanings to apparently irrational and supernatural fantasies in a way that Walpole or any of his disciples in the tradition of the Gothic romance of terror did not anticipate in the eighteenth and nineteenth centuries.

As *The Castle of Otranto* literally began in a dream, we feel justified in interpreting this tale as one, particularly as a vividly detailed wish-fulfillment dream that expresses the author's unconscious and ambivalent hopes and fears. "Visions," he wrote to Montagu, January 5, 1766, "have always been my pasture. . . . In short, you have opened a new landscape to my fancy. . . . I don't know, but the idea may produce some other Castle of Otranto." That Walpole himself delighted in this escapist fantasy, he confesses to Mme du Deffand on March 13, 1767, thus suggesting a freely operating pleasure principle; and what he himself said about it in that letter as an irrational work in which he gave "reins to [his] imagination till [he] became on fire with the visions and feeling which it entailed" demonstrates that here, too, he deliberately released himself from a conscious censor, removed his mask, and permitted us a brief but revealing glimpse into his unconscious mind.

II   *The Horror of Incest:* The Mysterious Mother

Walpole had "thought often on the subject" of tragedy and had developed his taste for it by much critical reading in the genre. Apart from Shakespeare, whose natural genius he insisted was above the rules of the drama, he admired Thomas Otway and Thomas Southerne, and specifically John Dryden's *All for Love* and *Don Sebastian*; Nicholas Rowe's *Fair Penitent* and *Jane Shore,* which he considered a perfect tragedy, and Edward Young's *Revenge.* He ranked the works of Racine, Corneille, and Voltaire above all English tragedies except that of Shakespeare, although he did object to "a fantastic decorum, that does not exist in nature," in the French. It is surprising, in view of the militant rationalism of his own play, *The Mysterious Mother,* to note his dislike of Voltaire's *Zaire*; for along with *Alzire, Mahomet,* and *Semiramis,* Walpole's play ranks with the plays of Voltaire which attack religious fanaticism. However, Walpole did admit that these three tragedies were his favorites. Walpole also thought that writing a good tragedy was easier than writing a good comedy (he means a comedy of manners): both require equal genius, but in addition "a comedy demands a more uncommon assemblage of qualities—knowledge of the world, wit, good sense, etc." He advised Robert Jephson to try writing comedy for he held "a good comedy the *chef d'oeuvre* of human genius."[13]

But Walpole himself attempted only a slight one-act farce, *Nature Will Prevail: A Moral Entertainment* (1773), a fantasy with some evidence of the supernatural borrowed from Shakespeare's *Tempest,* about Current, a foolish incorrigible gossip; Padlock, a cautious, treacherous and cunning knave; Almadine, a charming fairy; and Finette, a pretty country girl. The moral reflects Walpole's personal preferences—that is, his disgust with Padlock who, betraying his friend, represents "caution, reserve, suspicion, cunning, self-interest and treachery."[14] On the other hand, loquacious people may be fools, but then they possess the magic that wins pretty girls. A trifling bit of fluff, the play is interesting because it associates with our picture of Walpole as a scandalmonger and because it employs the supernatural, thereby illustrating Walpole's delight in fantasy. Obviously, however, Walpole was more successful with tragedy than comedy.

The Mysterious Mother, his tragedy in heroic blank verse, represents Walpole's greatest poetical and dramatic effort. He himself thought, rather immodestly, that this play demonstrated his talent for tragedy.[15] With it, as with *The Castle of Otranto,* he wanted to do something new—to write a play of great passion in order to shake the British theater out of the doldrums in which, in his opinion, it was languishing. Thus he did not soften the harsh tragic tone of this play with any comic interludes. Although he did not think Shakespeare's mixing of comedy with tragedy was a violation of propriety, and in the second preface to *Otranto* justified this practice by referring to Shakespeare's precedent, he admits no such softening in *The Mysterious Mother*. Nor could he allow a happy ending; for, as he wrote, he detested the current tragicomedies, "those gross and barbarous productions."[16]

Indeed, *The Mysterious Mother* is as pure and unrelieved a tragedy of suffering as one could find in the eighteenth century. It lacks contrasting light touches—all is invariably harsh and gloomy, and far more intensely passionate, far more powerful, than anything in *Otranto*. As Walpole writes in the Postscript to the play, the evocation of terror and pity was of foremost importance to him, far more significant than the mechanic rules of the drama—the three unities, the justness of the moral, and the probability of the situation and the behavior and motivation of the characters—all of which, incidentally, Walpole is careful to observe anyway:

From the time that I first undertook the foregoing scenes, I never flattered myself that they would be proper to appear on the stage. The subject is so horrid, that I thought it would shock rather than give satisfaction to an audience. Still I found it so truly tragic in the two essential springs of terror and pity, that I could not resist the impulse of adapting it to the scene, though it should never be practicable to produce it there. (*Works*, I, 125)

In the Prologue to the play, he writes in the same vein, declaring that the scene of the play is "horrid, not polite," and that he has not been intimidated by the rules. He appeals to Shakespeare, nature, and invention for freedom of expression; and he describes his play as a "Tremendous picture of domestic woe."[17] These remarks in the Prologue and Postscript resemble the prefaces to *Otranto* in one respect; for, as he explains and justifies his dramatic composition, we detect a curious paradox—the timidity with which he approaches Classical critical tenets is followed by a compulsive application of them to a sensationally romantic work of art.

Walpole, in this tightly structured play, builds up suspense carefully to the catastrophe at the very end, thereby demonstrating his mastery of stagecraft. The time of *The Mysterious Mother* is the dawn of the

Reformation. The Countess of Narbonne loved her husband passionately and was separated from him for a year and a half. On September 20, just as he returns home to the castle, he is killed by a ferocious stag, and his bloody corpse is presented to the horrified woman. Meanwhile, her son, Edmund, had arranged an assignation with his mother's handmaid Beatrice on the same night. The Countess, offended that he should have thought of amorous intrigue at such a tragic time, determines to meet him herself in place of Beatrice, in order to reprove him. However, the situation is too much for her: the passionate and sensual widow believes she sees in her son the image of his father. Grief, disappointment, and opportunity do the rest. But Edmund does not know that he has had intercourse with his mother. And so, a child is conceived, the young woman Adeliza, an orphan whom the Countess raises as her ward in a neighboring convent. This is the mystery that is preserved until the very end of the play.

Horrified by her own behavior, the Countess is unable to bear the presence of her son. Accusing him of impiety, of profaning his father's memory, she banishes Edmund from Narbonne, giving his affair with Beatrice as the palpable reason for her hostility. However, she generously continues to support him during his exile. After sixteen years of soldiering, Edmund becomes weary of his vagrant life and returns to Narbonne to regain his patrimony. Of course, he meets sweet young Adeliza with whom he promptly falls in love.

It is at this point, three weeks after he meets the girl, that the play's stage action begins—on the anniversary of his father's death and also of the passionate night of love with his mother. Because Father Benedict wishes to gain control of Narbonne's wealth and power, and to avenge the insults directed at his church by the Countess's Voltairean skepticism, and because he suspects the truth and guesses "her fatal secret" that Adeliza is really the Countess's daughter begot in some unlawful manner, the arch-villain priest marries them. Thereupon, the Countess becomes "wild" and confesses her monstrous crime to her son: she admits she is his mother and mistress, and "the mother of thy [Edmund's] daughter, sister, wife!" The girl faints; the mother kills herself. At the end, the son banishes Adeliza to a convent, returns to war as a relief, and leaves the Narbonne inheritance in possession of the church.

The same mind and imagination, it is clear, conceived both fantasies—*The Castle of Otranto*, and *The Mysterious Mother*, and the critical materials accompanying each work. In the criticism associated with these works, Walpole declares that terror and pity are the two principal instruments of effective writing; that it is desirable to keep the reader's attention up to the climax of the catastrophe; that the servants must be treated naturally and in marked contrast with the heroes and princes (and he had copied Shakespeare in this respect); that his theme was retribution, distributive justice, remorse, following upon the idea that the sins of parents are visited upon their children; and that an artful priest or monk play a significant role in some relationship with a lord (but in *Otranto* it should be noted, Father Jerome, unlike Father Benedict, is gentle, virtuous, truly humane). All these notions are illustrated in both compositions.

Both works also sustain a Gothic atmosphere of mystery and terror, produced basically by an antique and gloomy castle that is cursed by a secret sin. Superstitions and miraculous events are associated with different things; in the novel, the monument to Alphonso, which bleeds; in the play, a cross erected to the memory of the Count, which is destroyed by a bolt of lightning. The ghost of Alphonso haunts his castle at Otranto; and the Count's ghost, with "clotted locks and eyes like burning skins," haunts the church porch at Narbonne. The play presents another version of Gothic terror; Walpole is right to say (in the Epilogue, 1–2) that his "head is fill'd with Gothic fancies, and teems with ghosts, and giants and romances," although he places the action during an epoch later than the Dark Ages.

The full meaning of this play is expressed in two themes, both of which were highly personal and of great significance to Walpole: rational religion and incest. With regard to the first, Walpole certainly projected his religious beliefs into the general situation and the characters of this play. For example, the tragic heroine, the Countess of Narbonne, is, like her creator, a rationalist and Deist. She inveighs against monkish superstition and berates the wicked priest Benedict when he asks her to consult "a holy man" who has performed miracles to cure her mysterious despair:

> . . . Shall he teach me charms and spells,
> To make my sense believe against my sense?
> Shall I think practices and penances
> Will, if he say so, give the health of virtue
> To gnawing self-reproach?—I know they cannot. . . .
> We want no preacher to distinguish vice
> From virtue. At our birth the god reveal'd
> All conscience needs to know. . . . Weak minds
> Want their soul's fortune told by oracles
> And holy jugglers. . . . (I, v, 55)[18]

She insists that good deeds can improve the state of her soul and "penance cleanse it to receive the blessing" (III, iii, 82); therefore, she deliberately rejects the absolution that she could secure by confessing her sin to the priest. In the Postscript Walpole defends his heavy emphasis on "the sublimity of sense and reason in the character of the Countess" and insists that his stress on the Countess's rationalism in an age of superstition does not lack probability. He thought that it was not necessarily certain that she become a superstitious enthusiast because of "the excess of her repentence," a view held by his critics. His argument against this opinion is "that virtue could and ought to leave more lasting stings in a mind conscious of having fallen; and that weak minds alone believe or feel that conscience is to be lulled asleep by the incantations of bigotry" (I, 127). The Countess certainly is a woman with a strong mind. Besides, he adds, as the action occurred after the medieval period, "at the dawn of the reformation," she might have had assistance from the religious reformers of the time.

Whatever the probability of her characterization, it is obvious that the Countess does not trust the priests—and with good reason, since they are corrupt. Her skepticism, rationalism, and natural piety are supported by a healthy plain-speaking minor character, the soldier Florian, confidant of the hero Edmund. Florian, too, scorns the priests and challenges their authority: "Monks may reach heav'n, but never came from thence" (II, ii, 66). Disgusted by superstitious belief, he objects to "the saucy superiority of bigot pride" and "enthusiasm" (II, v, 74); and he candidly expresses his freethinking as he describes the period of Edmund's banishment in terms of the militant and secular eighteenth-century Enlightenment:

> . . . These sixteen years
> Has my friend Edmund pin'd in banishment
> While masses, mummings, goblins and processions
> Usurp'd his heritage, and made of Narbonne
> A theatre of holy interludes
> And sainted frauds. But day darts on your spells.
> Th'enlighten'd age eschews your vile deceits,
> And truth shall do mankind and Edmund justice.
>
> (V, iii, 111)

In effect, Walpole makes the Countess a Protestant, as she persistently uses her private reason (so Benedict complains) and refuses to go to confession. Even in the Epilogue, he calls her "a methodist." A woman of lofty principles, she devotes her life to good works. She is a strong-minded independent personality, stoical and austere, and inspiring awe. "Ten such," the nasty Benedict is made to say, "would unbuild our Roman church." The priest obviously recognizes the tremendous intensity and sincerity of her devotion (I, iii, 45). She even leans toward "the singing saints of Savoy's neighboring vale," the heretical Waldenses, or Vaudois, against whom the church was preparing a horribly destructive crusade (IV, i, 91).

When the agony of keeping her secret to herself eventually unhinges her reason, Walpole's anti-Catholic message again comes through clearly. For right reason is overwhelmed by dark and evil superstition: the good woman is driven over the brink into hysteria and madness by religious but malevolent and sadistic psychopaths, who, fathoming her secret, deliberately against all decency and morality marry her son and daughter to each other. Thereby the diabolical priests have succeeded in destroying her, as well as her family, in accordance with their chief objectives, as the wicked Benedict openly declares: "I cannot dupe, and therefore must destroy her:/Involve her house in ruin so prodigious,/ That neither she nor Edmund may survive it" (IV, i, 91).

To support his view of the Countess, Walpole's attitude toward the two Roman Catholic priests, Benedict and Martin, is consistently hostile, an attitude fostered by his own Deistic rationalism and strong personal prejudice against papists and superstition. These two he satirically portrays as "meddling monks . . . paid for being saints" (I, ii; V, ii), who encourage superstition in order to aggrandize their power (IV, i, 90–91). Walpole must have taken a keen delight in his presentation of these crafty, depraved creatures, the arch-villain Benedict and his weaker brother and confidant Martin, because they so positively confirm his personal bias. Of the two "grim enthusiasts,"[19] Benedict is far more vicious and dangerous: in the Postscript Walpole declares that "the villainy of Benedict was planned to divide the indignation of the audience, and to intercept some of it from the Countess. Nor will the blackness of his character appear extravagant, if we call to mind the crimes commited by catholic churches, when the reformation not only provoked their rage, but threatened them with total ruin."[20] He is drawn as a shrewd and sinister hypocrite with a twisted mind; as he himself admits, he is not even "an honest bigot" (I, iii, 48).

Ambitious to become a cardinal and to advance the church by destroying the Countess, Benedict loses every humane virtue: "For her," Walpole makes him say, "each virtue from my breast I banish" (IV, i, 90). Indeed, portrayed as so despicably unscrupulous, he has even lost his faith, being really devoted, like the satanic Iago, to evil, revenge, and sadistic cruelty. But Walpole generally puts Benedict's motivation within a Deistic framework, which suggests the cause of his hostility: since the Countess rejects, as Benedict declares, "Our Roman church . . . our beads, our hymns, our saints" (I, iii, 45), since she and her son are "thinking heretics" and "must reason," they cannot be spared (IV, i, 90). An unscrupulous Machiavellian villain without a single redeeming virtue, a hateful melodramatic grotesque straight out of hell, Father Benedict contributes to the Gothic atmosphere of the play. In the history of Gothic literature, this criminal monk is closely allied to the tyrant type, assimilating the generally outward characteristics of that sombre and terrifying hero.

Rationalism, as we have noted, is the chief attribute of the Countess—particularly of her consciousness which is represented symbolically by daylight; at night, however, she appears to be an altogether different woman. A demon-lover, perhaps, or a witch, she is driven, possessed, completely irrational as she succumbs to a powerful unconscious drive and seduces her son. Such is the unsavoury incest which Walpole paradoxically develops along with religious rationalism. The theme of incest was soon to be favored by Gothic authors because it was easily adaptable to the evocation of thrilling horror; but Walpole's generation had reservations about it, for precisely this "intrinsic fault in the choice of the subject," this shocking breach of a powerful taboo, makes *The Mysterious Mother,* as Walpole sadly confessed to Jephson, "a tragedy that never can appear on any stage."[21]

In his Postscript he tries to justify the choice of a "subject . . . so horrid" by insisting on the moral directed against "an unbounded passion." But this statement is a mere rationalization deriving from the surface level of consciousness. Certainly, the reason for Walpole's powerful attraction to this story material goes far deeper than this remark indicates. For despite its shocking and indelicate character, he himself says he "could not resist the impulse of adapting it to the scene," nor could he destroy it. He refused to accept the bowdlerizing emendations of his friend William Mason and had fifty copies printed in 1768 on his own press to fix the text just as he wanted it, undistorted and undiluted; and thirteen years later, in order to prevent any pirating or corrupting, he permitted Dodsley to publish it in London. Furthermore, "when very young," he writes, he had heard of a similar story from real life. We recall, also, that in *The Castle of Otranto* there is a strong hint of incest in Manfred's plan to marry his dead son's

fiancée, a plan that the good friar Jerome thwarts.[22] Clearly, we are
justified in asking why at this time of life, Walpole found a story of a
woman's deliberate violation of a fundamental taboo so irresistible,
even though unpardonable and "disgusting," and why, at the same
time, he associated this impulse with a memory of childhood.[23]

Of course, it is inevitable that he compare his work with Sophocles'
King Oedipus. In the Postscript, he shows that he is aware that his
"subject is more truly horrid than even that of Oedipus." In the Greek
play, he points out, ignorance and coincidence determine the outcome
and palliate the crimes of incest and parricide. But in his play, Walpole
bases the action upon frank and uncontrollable passion, incest
committed prepense. He boldly projects on to the mother sexual desire
for her son, and only in the course of the play does he extenuate her
willful criminal passion in an agonizing remorse. Throughout, the poor
Countess appears extremely contrite, sensitive, humane, pious yet
unbigoted—an attractive and imposing tragic figure suffering from a
painful and mysterious guilt complex.

Thus as Walpole appears to explain and excuse the crime he raises
the character of the criminal and makes her deserving of pity. To make
the situation even more satisfying to his mental state, Walpole puts
practically all the blame for the tragedy that transpires—the destruction
of the whole family of Narbonne—on the evil influence of psychopathic
Romish priests, a terrifying anti-Catholic obsession developed in his
formative years. Therefore, because Walpole attempts to soften the
impact of the incestuous situation, we may properly ask if it is possible
to read *The Mysterious Mother,* like *The Castle of Otranto,* as a
disturbing nightmarish fantasy—what Freud calls a punishment dream—
and as a typical Oedipal family romance with a highly personal,
although unconscious, meaning for the writer.

In the three-year interval between the composition and publication
of his two Gothic fancies, Walpole continued his close relationship with
Conway, despite a near rupture because of his cousin's offensive
coldness and insensibility. Walpole also began, in his first visit to Paris
from August 1765 to April 1766, a warm relationship with Mme du
Deffand. He began the composition of the play Christmas Day of 1766
and completed it on March 15, 1768.

Conway, it will be remembered, had been dismissed from the king's
service for his opposition to General Warrants. Walpole was so agitated
by the mistreatment of Conway that he withdrew to Strawberry Hill
and, driven by his unconscious, composed a wish fulfillment fantasy,
The Castle of Otranto, in which his hero emerges triumphant. In July, a

year later, however, a new ministry was formed because of the king's displeasure with the Regency Bill. Rockingham became the chief minister, and Conway one of the secretaries of state and the leader of the House of Commons. All that Walpole had struggled for was accomplished—Grenville and Bedford were dismissed; Rockingham and Conway of the opposition were supreme. But Walpole was not made entirely happy by this event because of Conway's insensitivity and ingratitude. Conway made no effort to reward Walpole's loyalty, a neglect that Walpole considered an unpardonable insult. To escape from the bitterness of this traumatic experience, Walpole, despite Conway's pleas that he remain in England to help him, felt alienated and banished himself to Paris, where he soon met Mme du Deffand and soothed his battered ego. Upon his return to England, however, he buried his resentment and remained in close political contact with his cousin, serving as his most trusted counselor and guide.

However, when on January 20, 1768, Conway resigned his seals of office, it was against Walpole's wishes. This painful event may have precipitated his conclusive withdrawal from Parliament, although he had promised himself and others to quit that assembly before. Thus, again, Walpole banished himself and thereby punished himself as well as Conway. If we also recall that Conway was always associated in Walpole's mind with his mother, thereby unconsciously generating a feeling of guilt, we can understand how these traumatic events reflected symbolically in the play (that is, in Edmund's banishment from the castle and the Countess's self-punishment) contributed to the compulsive choice of the theme of incest.

On the latent level of the play, then, Conway represents the mother surrogate; and his denial clearly provides grounds for an unpleasant traumatic situation. In the tragic fantasy into which Walpole unconsciously projected his thoughts, this idea is represented by the son's achieving an erotic relationship with his mother after his father is killed, resulting in painful guilt and his punishment in alienation and exile. The ultimate psychological causes of Walpole's effort to punish himself in order to alleviate his guilt are exhibited in the wish-fulfillment dream realized in the fictional *Otranto,* which ties in with Conway's success on the political scene in 1765. In this fiction, the son Theodore achieves all his desires, marries the lovely woman, and inherits the castle, all at the expense of the father Manfred, who, mutilated, is thereupon relegated to a convent. But in life such a solution was not satisfactory, for it unconsciously represented the gratification of forbidden impulses, parricide and incest. Hence renunciation, punishment, and atonement must be enacted upon the unconscious violation of these terrifying moral taboos.

Similarly, Walpole's relationship with Mme du Deffand was somewhat ambivalent. Her devotion was satisfying; but it also was humiliating, disconcerting, and embarrassing because it represented a gratification of hidden impulses—the elderly sixty-nine-year-old woman, twenty years Walpole's senior, unconsciously personified his protective mother. The woman herself recognized the filial nature of his affection for her: "Je serai votre mère," she said once; and, before his second visit, she was calling him her son.[24]

The result of such a psychological situation is comparable to the conflict between guilt and pleasure that Walpole experienced in his association with Conway. To assuage the sense of guilt arising from the inner condemnation of acts which symbolically realize definite wish-impulses, denial, renunciation, and punishment are necessary. So Walpole's self-punishment in his relationship with the old blind woman was accomplished through his refusal to accept and enjoy her love. His defensive scoldings and prohibitions (he told her, for example, never to use the word *love* in her letters to him) signify that he was transferring his guilt to the infatuated woman. That is to say, she was responsible for this embarrassing situation; he was simply the innocent recipient of her affectionate addresses; he was the person who suffered the possible ridicule as decently and patiently as he could.

Other symbolizations and projections confirm the viability of this psychological approach to the play. To illustrate this generalization, the character of the Countess may be cited. As we have intimated, the initial incest between the Countess and her son represents an extension of Walpole's devotion and allegiance to his mother Lady Walpole. The Countess's piety, like that of gentle and long-suffering Hippolita of *Otranto,* supports this notion. This charitable woman, portrayed as superhuman, supervirtuous, absolutely just (I, iii, 42, 45, 49), parallels the youthful Walpole's exaggerated overvaluation of his mother. At the same time, this union between mother and son reflects the current association between Mme du Deffand and Walpole, the older woman using the younger man to mitigate the loneliness, the spiritual sterility and vacuity of her existence. Nor is it surprising to see that the chief character traits of the Countess resemble those of Mme de Deffand: both are sensual, skeptical, and rational, yet environed by a religious atmosphere—the French woman living in the secular portion of the Convent of St. Joseph. The Countess thus appears as a strange composite of Lady Walpole and the French marquise: virtuous, pious, skeptical, rational, and passionately sensual. With regard to remorse, however, the case is different. This motif which expresses the latent psychological theme of the play derives from Walpole himself, from his current relationship with Conway and Mme du Deffand which triggered a profoundly unconscious remorse for an infantile fantasy concerning the destruction of his father, forbidden wishes that were exposed and realized in the conclusion of *Otranto,* and in the play before the stage action begins (the killing of the father by the stag providing the opportunity for incest with the mother).

Furthermore, the use of numbers in this play is strangely significant. Events radiate sixteen years before and after the date of September 20—the date when the Count (the father) is killed, the incest with the Countess (the mother) occurs, the action of the play begins with the return of the son to his ancestral home and ends with her death by suicide. These two numbers—sixteen and twenty—may be considered screening symbols that allude to repressed material in the unconscious mind. On September 20, Sir Robert Walpole's favorite sister Dolly, wife of Lord Townshend, gave birth to Walpole's cousin George Townshend, four days prior to Walpole's own arrival.[25] Walpole's birthday was unconsciously repressed because it tied him too obviously with the incestuous theme; but the cousin's birthday had no intelligible connection with the forbidden motif. On January 20, 1768, Conway resigned the seals of his office as secretary of state and gave the lead in the Commons to Lord North, precipitating Walpole's farewell to Parliament. Again, the number twenty is the exact difference in years between Walpole and Mme du Deffand. Also, Lady Walpole had died on August 20, about thirty years before. The number, therefore, brings to mind the anniversary of her death and equates with the day on which the Countess dies. Lastly, with respect to this idea, as W. S. Lewis has indicated, the positioning of Walpole's tender epitaph on Lady Walpole, with its praise of her sensibility, charity, purity, and unbigoted piety, *immediately after* the Postscript of the play in the collected *Works* (I, 131) that Walpole himself arranged for posthumous publication, suggests the force of Walpole's incestuous impulse. Thus, Walpole transmutes these personal associations that are tied with powerful instinctual drives into indifferent material and, at the same time, with typical psychological ambivalence, expresses and conceals them.

In the same way the number sixteen is significant. After sixteen years, the banished Edmund returns home "shame-stricken" to his mother (II, i, 59–61), and in a long speech expresses ambivalent feelings for his mother whom he blames and mourns, loves and respects, and whose harshness and cruelty he resents, whose woes he pities. Detecting her suffering and anxiety, he wishes to comfort her and to ask her forgiveness. This speech expresses the spirit of Walpole's well-known nostalgic letter to Montagu (March 30, 1761) about his return home to Houghton Hall, also after sixteen years! In the letter Walpole writes of his dead parents—his mother in "yonder church—that church, into which I have not yet had courage to enter, where lies the mother on whom I doted, and who doted on me!" He thinks of his father who "sleeps in quiet and dignity." Sadly, penitentially, and unconsciously, he assumes the role of his father—as we have noted in the discussion of Houghton.

To conclude, the number sixteen becomes a clue pointing directly to Walpole's intimate connection with the theme of remorse and revenge; and, through the shielding figure of Edmund who returns home after sixteen years, Walpole gives voice to his own poignant recollections of the past. The outcome of the play, which illustrates a retaliatory catastrophic obliteration for the criminal destruction of the father, suggests that it is a penitential offering. Thus at its conclusion, as the father takes his revenge and appears to be triumphant, Walpole, it may be said, lays to rest guilty yearnings which were exposed in the dream of *Otranto*. When one of the priests cries, "Heav'n vindicates its altars" (II, ii, 68–69; V, i, 106), the father figure is magnified into the symbolical all-powerful heavenly father who punishes the sinners for their awful crimes.

Symbolism in *The Mysterious Mother* provides additional evidence to support this interpretation of the unconscious theme. Many of the symbols of latent erotic significance in *Otranto* are employed in the dramatic sequel: the dagger, the cross, the Count's monument, the Count's specter flying in the whirlwind, the castle, and the chapel. In the novel, Manfred loses control of the sexual tokens which are passed on to the victorious son; but, in the play, the rapacious father figures, the two monks, vanquish mother and son. Thus the cross (male emblem) erected by the Countess is destroyed by a bolt of lightning aimed by the specter (II, iii, 70), and the "shield of arms" (female emblem) is also "shivered to splinters" (II, ii, 68) under this violent attack. In addressing the ghost, the Countess voluntarily offers "her destin'd head," thereby suggesting the mutilation motif. Moreover, a violent deed performed in a chapel concludes both works: the dagger, when mistakenly plunged into Matilda's breast, causes Manfred's destruction; but in the play "a poor friar's knife" fells his enemies' "tow'ring grandeur to the earth" (V, i, 106), and the Countess stabs herself, whereupon the son is again banished, and Adeliza, like Manfred, is enclosed in a convent. The Narbonne family thus destroyed, the castle is possessed by the fathers. The details of this final scene clearly exhibit on a symbolic level, the ritual of atonement. The deprived and defeated father of the preceding fantasy is in the sequel restored to his triumphant position of power: the secret sin has been exposed; the agonizing guilt is painfully purged away.

Such may be the uniquely personal and universal elements dramatized in *The Mysterious Mother*. Because Walpole seriously attempted to treat incest as a tragic subject rather than as a device for achieving cheap sensationalism, the play generates a good deal of dramatic power. Walpole put more of himself into this work than he was aware, and this may be the reason for the effect of the play upon its readers. Thus Manfred and especially the Countess appear to come to life as they take on an added dimension. The drama of Narbonne, like the narrative of Otranto, is a fascinating psychological palimpsest wherein the outlines of the author's life at a time of crisis may be deciphered. It may not be wrong to declare that whatever strange attraction both works will continue to exert is attributable to their haunting erotic archetypes and Gothic grotesquerie.

III   *Troubled Dreams:* Hieroglyphic Tales

"Apprehensive lest the work should be lost to posterity," as Walpole wrote with mock gravity in his preface, he had the *Hieroglyphic Tales* printed on his press in 1785, only seven copies of a collection of six fantasies.[26] The first was written in August, 1766, and the remainder between 1770 and 1772 apparently for the amusement of his little female friends, Miss Caroline Campbell, eldest daughter of Lord William Campbell, who lived with her aunt, the Countess of Ailesbury (Conway's wife); and Lady Anne Fitzpatrick, daughter of the countess of Upper Ossory, with whom Walpole carried on an extensive correspondence. No doubt, Walpole hoped that their parents and older friends would read them, too. Some of these "strange" fairy tales, "even wilder than *The Castle of Otranto*," he wrote to Cole, January 28, 1779, do exceed in their extravagance anything in the romantic novel, even the deployment of sections of Alphonso's gigantic limbs. In this letter to Cole, Walpole also declared, lest his friends have the wrong idea, that the stories were not written when he was ill "in the gout, nor whatever they may seem, written when I was out of my senses."

In his preface, Walpole imagines that these short stories "were undoubtedly written a little before the creation of the world, and have ever since been preserved, by oral tradition, in the mountains of Crampcraggiri, an uninhabited land, not yet discovered."[27] He mentions the probability that they were composed by Kemanrlegorpikos, son of Quat, or Quat's nurse, or Hermes Trismegistus. These speculations establish the tone of the work and define the proper attitude in which Walpole wished the stories to be read. As one of his notes indicates, "The merit of an Hierogylphic Tale consists in its being written extempore and without any plan, as the four first of these litteraly [*sic*] were."[28]

His intention, as he also explains in his postscript to the collection, is to introduce fancy, variety, and novelty to "writings in which the imagination is fettered by no rules, and by no obligation of speaking truth": "they are mere whimsical trifles, written chiefly for private entertainment; and for private amusement half a dozen copies only are printed. They deserve, at most, to be considered as an attempt to vary the stale and beaten class of stories and novels, which, though works of invention, are almost always devoid of imagination."[29]

Composing some of these stories automatically, Walpole writes more seriously than he consciously admits. As will be seen, the crazy tales reveal in devious ways the irritants and obsessions that troubled Walpole's mind. They are by no means merely pretty, delicate, or airy fantasies written with the innocence of a childish spirit. But there are degrees of seriousness, grades of fun, in the collection—the stories range from sheer nonsense and healthy comedy, to coarse and gross indecency and sick laughter; from crude anticlerical to somewhat shrewd political satire. References to real people and events abound—and these may be, especially in the first four stories, not quite so delicate or refined as we should expect from a writer of Walpole's exquisite sensibility. Indeed, Walpole took care that some of his references should not be missed. He annotated one copy so that posterity might know that he was gibing at a departed monarch, or at the monarch then reigning and at his chief minister (George III and Lord Bute), or at the figure of a reigning beauty (the duchess of Kingston, Miss Chudleigh), or at the brainlessness of a lord chancellor (Henry Bathurst, Lord Apsley).[30]

In the first tale, "A New Arabian Nights Entertainment," Walpole writes of the clever Princess Gronovia who keeps the Emperor of Cucurucu awake all night with her prating. She is supposed to be beheaded after she completes her story in the morning. However, when the king himself finally falls asleep, she smothers him and becomes ruler of the country. In the course of the narrative, Walpole scatologically ridicules royal flatterers, Jesuits, Calvinists, and Richard Glover, author of the soporific epic *Leonidas*. The satire is tangential, for Walpole never lingers long enough to develop his ideas—to become either dull or penetrating.

There is, of course, on the simple level of logic, or the lack of it, a good deal of amusing clowning nonsense in some of the tales. For example, the Princess Gronovia begins her adventures by attempting to gather goat's eggs; and in the second of these stories, "the King and His Three Daughters," there is a king with three daughters, the eldest of whom was never born! This eldest daughter is chosen to be the bride of Quifferiquimini "who would have been the most accomplished hero of the age, if he had not been dead, and had spoken any language but the Egyptian, and had not three legs." All goes as well as could be expected until the two royal houses quarrel about religion, Calvinist grace, and the papacy.

It is curious, in view of Walpole's apparent obsession with the theme of incest, that this also should become a problem, for, as it turns out, the two parties are too closely related: "it was . . . necessary to have a dispensation from the pope, the parties being related within the forbidden degrees; a woman that never was, and a man that had been, being deemed first cousins in the eye of the canon law."[31] "Who the devil would have married your-no-daughter, but a dead body!" cries the infuriated corpse. And in the end he was given a "pompous funeral" and buried "in spite of his appeal to the law of nations." Flavoring these surrealistic, ghoulish details is a dash of satire on political factions and ridiculous religious doctrines.

The third fairy tale, "The Dice Box," is about a little girl Pissimissi who is pulled around the world in the shell of a pistachio nut drawn by an elephant and a ladybird. After many nonsensical adventures, all are swallowed by a giant hummingbird who carries them to his master, King Solomon. After the king removes them from the bird's gullet, he is inspired to begin the Song of Songs "extempore." However, the Queen of Sheba, jealous of Pissimissi, plasters a dice box on the girl's flattened nose: "it stuck there, and being of ivory, Solomon ever after compared his beloved's nose to the tower that leads to Damascus." Thereupon, the queen furiously drives away and is never heard of again. Once more, readers sense—in certain details about an unknown duchess's (Miss Chudleigh's) "beautiful breasts" that are compared to large sugar plums or about a woman's flat nose, and the light skeptical treatment of the imagery of Solomon's canticles—that Walpole is not addressing these stories merely to innocent children, but also to their knowing parents or relatives. At the same time, too, he provides some insights into the compulsions of his own prankish psyche.

The fourth tale, "The Peach in Brandy," takes the prize for poor taste, unless eighteenth-century men and women were far less squeamish than people today. Walpole says that this story was written for "Anne Liddell, Countess of Ossory, wife of John Fitzpatrick, Earl of Ossory. They had a daughter Anne, the subject of this tale." The story was included in a letter to the girl's father, December 4, 1771, in which Walpole describes it as "this foolery." How foolish it is we shall presently see. The Countess had, according to Walpole's own note, just then "miscarried of twins," two boys. Another note tells of "the housekeeper, [who], as soon as Lord Ossory came home, wished him joy of a son and heir, though both the children were born dead."[32] The point is that the Countess had three daughters by Ossory and failed to give him the son he desired. Walpole's story ends with the male embryo, which is preserved in brandy, being mistaken for a peach and gulped down by the Roman Catholic Archbishop of Tuum who is suffering from a violent fit of the colic. (Incidentally, this bishop is also accused, out of the blue, of committing incest with his sister!)

It is hard to believe that Walpole's good friend could be entertained by such a nauseating conclusion, much less her three-year-old daughter Lady Anne. The delightful verses that Walpole addressed to the little girl with a present of shells (1772) are in far better—or more nearly normal—taste, and are far more appropriate to what most adults think their children may favor. But obviously this grisly tale, meant to needle the frustrated Ossorys, succeeds only in becoming a hideous joke. How well they took it remains a mystery.

The last two tales have an altogether different quality than that of the preceding four. These suggest daylight; the others, darkness. "Mi Li: A Chinese Fairy Tale" tells of the search by a prince for "a princess whose name was the same with her father's dominions." The young prince, after searching around the world, is eventually led to Park Place, the Berkshire seat of General Conway's country home, which gives Walpole the opportunity to satirize good humoredly fashionable gardening practices which Conway adopted—a subterranean passage with gleaming rocks, "a heap of artificial ruins," "a stupendous bridge" which "had not a drop of water beneath it," and "a lonely tomb" where nobody was buried nor ever would be buried, which Walpole describes in a note as "a fictitious tomb in a beautiful spot by the river, built for a point of view: it has a small pyramid on it."³³ All these features of the romantic garden Walpole himself favored.

At Park Place, the prince finds his princess in little Caroline Campbell, the niece of Conway and his wife Lady Ailesbury, and the daughter of Lord William Campbell, late governor of the American province of Carolina. Of all the stories, this is the most innocuous, the most charming. The reason is easy to see: it does not include any objectionable, grimly macabre, details. "Mi Li" lacks, therefore, any sense of nightmare vision that characterizes the preceding tales.

The very last tale, "A True Love Story," is about the love of Orondates for Azora, an exquisitely beautiful African slave, but the affair is frustrated because of the aversion of their mistresses for each other. The abbess who owned Azora, a prude and a bigot, attempted to prevent their marriage with blows and threats; she so terrified poor Azora that the slave fell into labor and miscarried—four puppies! (This story, like the fourth, was also sent Lady Ossory, February 6, 1780!) So we learn with surprise that Orondates is an Italian greyhound and Azora, a black spaniel. In the characterization of the wicked abbess, Walpole's religious hostility again peeks through. Except for details that reflect Walpole's anti-Catholic bias and a tasteless harping on miscarriages, this story, like the preceding fantasy on gardening fashions, is good for a little laugh.

A strong psychological compulsion to be whimsical made Walpole indulge his capacity for fantasy. Some of the nonsense stories in this collection of *Hieroglyphic Tales,* the first four in particular, bring to mind the uncanny extravaganzas of surrealism, differing from Gothic supernaturalism and terror only in the lightness of the tone. From time to time, however, these apparently trifling stories introduce visions that are weird and ghastly, and irony so severely caustic, that the reader cannot help sensing something very disturbing in the author's inner nature. Mme du Deffand, who had read the first three stories, thought Walpole mad and his work the result of delirium or dreams (April 3, 1772). We wonder what her reaction to the fourth would have been.

Walpole denied that he was mad when he wrote these fantasies, but the French woman's insight penetrated close to the real truth, as she noted the dreamlike quality of the three early stories. Perhaps, like the dream of Otranto, they ought to be interpreted as evidences of the secret unconscious reflecting a profound dissatisfaction with life—as dreams that reveal infantile regressions. Thus, for example, Gronovia's climbing the mountain in search of goat's eggs is obvious erotic symbolism, and the whole story (including of course the several mutilation motifs and the death of the emperor, the father figure) reflects the same militantly aggressive egotism and infantile yearnings that appeared in *The Castle of Otranto.*

At any rate, many of the stories do exhibit a religious rationalist, obsessively and irreverently laughing at what he thought were the silly aberrations of rigorous Presbyterians or Calvinists and of bigoted Catholics, and an insensitive bachelor vulgarly smirking at unfortunate stillbirths and miscarriages.

These little stories, generally dismissed in Walpole criticism because of their fantastic irrationalism and apparently fluffy quality, could, just like his more conventional efforts in prose and verse, be explored seriously for evidences of the nature and content of the author's mind and imagination.

CHAPTER 5

A Measure of the Man and the Artist

HORACE WALPOLE is a controversial figure in history. After his death, he suffered a great loss of reputation—he was attacked for his barbaric behavior to Mme du Deffand; blamed for the early death of Chatterton; condemned for his Whig distortions of history; and, in general, belittled for being a cold-blooded, self-centered, affected trifler of the patrician class with no capacity for genuine feeling or for truly intellectual concerns. Today, too, his reputation is that of a dilettante who dabbled in the fine arts and a gossip who had a talent for writing letters. Yet Walpole has also had no dearth of sympathetic admirers who, coming to his defense, point to his prodigious literary output—his many contributions to literature, art, and history, and to his almost countless letters that provide intimate, vivid, and varied glimpses into sixty years of English life long ago.

Whatever the difficulty of providing final estimates and conclusive measures of a writer's achievement in order to fix his position securely in literary history, one thing is certain: the cross section of Horace Walpole's mind presented in this study reveals that his over-all achievement in several areas of thought and taste was by no means insignificant. As a writer of social, political, and art history, he has become an indispensable primary source of information. As an imaginative writer, he pioneered with the Gothic tale of terror and the Gothic drama. As an architect and a gardenist, he favored informal and natural landscapes and picturesque Gothic, thereby affecting the English vision and contributing to changing trends in taste. Lastly, as a literary personality in his own right, he is intrinsically interesting, for he has provided ample materials worthy of continuing critical consideration. Having written so much and so well throughout his long life, Walpole exhibited numerous facets of his changing personality. Inevitably he appears complex; and complex writers have the enduring virtue of arousing curiosity and thereby remaining alive—if only in the minds of their readers.

Considering his mental profile, the impression of its ambivalence is outstanding—hence, also, the essential complexity of the man and the difficulty of reaching conclusions acceptable to all readers of his works. Still, certain main lines do appear to be prominent, despite obscuring ambiguities.

What seems to be most engaging about Walpole is his humanism. This term, in the sense of his being a versatile man of letters with a liberal frame of mind, describes a quality that may be considered a constant in his religious and political thought. With regard to religion, it accounts for his Deism, skepticism, and rationalism, and his constant attacks upon bigotry and intolerance, superstition, and fanatical enthusiasm in whatever denomination, and, of course, especially in the two dominant churches of his time, Catholic and Episcopal. Nor could he abide the Methodists, whose "principles" he once tried to learn, as he wrote to Mann, July 24, 1749, from observing their ritual and reading their works: "The visible part seems to be nothing but stricter practice than that of our church, clothed in the old exploded cant of mystical devotion." On the other hand, appalled by the frankly espoused atheism of the French *Encyclopédistes,* he also thought that religious belief should not be undermined, and that the church in general served a useful function for the masses.

This cautious Deism parallels a cautious republicanism. True, he appeared to be outspoken in his Whig criticism of monarchy; but he really was, as he admitted, "quiet" about it. What this position meant in practice was constant opposition to any extension of the royal prerogative, so that in the course of normal attrition there would be a gradual erosion of the king's powers. Certainly, his thought was directed toward the supremacy of Parliament and the political liberty and democracy it structured in the next two centuries. However, whether he would have been pleased to see royalty become mere figureheads, the aristocracy destroyed, and only the middle and laboring classes competing for control of the state is another matter. We should never forget that Horace Walpole lived in the eighteenth century and belonged to the class of landowning magnates who shared the power with the king. If a Whig who wished to cut the king's claws, he was also one who took for granted the survival of the Whig oligarchy. To a great extent, this attitude, that of the so-called Old Whigs, may explain his reaction to the social revolution that the French National Assembly fomented, and that ushered in modern democracy. But, to him, the French appeared fanatically destructive; and so, under the circumstances, he felt compelled, as did many other rational men, to temper his republican and parliamentary sympathies according to his norms of reason, restraint, and tolerance. Liberty, he wrote to Mary Berry on July 9, 1790, might be bought too dearly: "No man living is more devoted to liberty than I am; yet blood is a terrible price to pay for it. A martyr to liberty is the noblest of characters; but to sacrifice the lives of others, though for the benefit of all, is a strain of heroism that I could never ambition." This is a humane criticism of a cruel and mechanic utilitarianism that goes to the heart of the matter. Undoubtedly, Walpole would have been pleased with the gradualism that characterizes the English political genius.

Allied with his humane and cautious religious rationalism and political Whiggism is his literary neo-Classicism. The overwhelming Classic image of Palladian Houghton, in a sense, suggests the kind of order and regularity he expected of art. Although he may have reacted against Houghton in order to assert his own personality when he Gothicized Strawberry Hill, Houghton permeated his being, influencing and determining his behavior and point of view more than he consciously knew. Thus it is not particularly surprising to see that when he was faced with the problem of structuring his two most important literary works, the popular *Castle of Otranto* and the passionate *Mysterious Mother,* he in a rather timid manner regressed and followed the old-fashioned Aristotelian blueprint for art. His critical justification of these highly imaginative and sensationally romantic creations is paradoxically conservative and Classical; and he is careful to control his imaginative fantasies and execute his literary maneuvers according to the craft rules and standards respected in his time.

Despite his rationalism and neo-Classicism, Walpole was often attracted to "magic" and fantasy. This romantic compulsion in his psyche explains his attraction to the supernatural, as in *The Castle of Otranto*; to the vision of passionate "gloomth," as in *The Mysterious Mother*; to the grotesque and surrealistic, as in *The Hieroglyphic Tales*; to the playfully imaginative, as in his delightful children's verse "To Lady Anne, when about Five Years Old, With a Present of Shells"; or to the faery caprice, as in *Nature Will Prevail.* The vision of the medieval past evoked by Strawberry Hill is allied to and reinforces this compulsion. The irregularity of this picturesque structure and the romantic garden designed for the grounds suggest the force of fantasy subject to no rule; and both obviously contradict neo-Classic order. Moreover, the Gothic quality of Strawberry Hill even suggests that superstition had its charms, for the irrational Gothic appealed to an imagination that was prepared to suspend disbelief and to respond sympathetically to the fantastically miraculous as an act of poetic faith. Thus, toward the end of his life, Walpole informed young Mary Berry on June 30, 1789, "There is a wildness [in the *Arabian Nights*] that captivates"; and he advised her to respect original genius, to "admire all bold and unique essays that resemble nothing else; [Erasmus Darwin's] *Botanic Garden*, the *Arabian Nights,* and King's College Chapel are above all rules."

Different levels in Walpole's mind reveal different and contradictory attitudes. Apparently extrovert, he led an intense public life which he cheerfully shared with others; and he put his house and the artifacts of his museum on exhibit. Such may be considered his life by day. But also apparently introvert, he had a private life which he sometimes shared with only a very few choice intimates or which he tried to keep entirely to himself. In solitude, he created his novel and play, and labored over his history of art and over his secret memoirs for almost as long a time as he continued to write letters. Perhaps even unknown to himself certain irrational obsessions and compulsions mysteriously motivated his behavior. His two most important imaginative works illuminate his unconscious or dream life and indicate the strategy whereby he was able to keep hidden his Oedipal impulses by means of various symbolic devices, psychological maneuvers, and subterfuges. Such may be considered his life at night. Again, many of his letters show him to be flippant and carefree, as he comments gaily on the glittering surface movements of eighteenth-century upper-class life. But this attitude of amused and aloof detachment is only on the surface of his being; for beneath this superficial level lies a profound and passionate commitment to art and politics which, disturbing him no end, may be considered the fundamental motives of his thought.

Furthermore, his political memoirs and his anecdotal letters testify to an intense and realistic commitment to the present. But he was also sentimentally and romantically attracted to dreams and visions of the past. Thus he wrote to Montagu, January 5, 1766,

Visions, you know, have always been my pasture; and so far from growing old enough to quarrel with their emptiness, I almost think there is no wisdom comparable to that of exchanging what is called the realities of life for dreams. Old castles, old pictures, old histories, and the babble of old people, make one live back into centuries that cannot disappoint one. One holds fast and surely what is past. The dead have exhausted their power of deceiving—one can trust Catherine of Medicis now.

Although the immediate cause of this poignant declaration of faith in the dead and the past may be found in a temporary mood of disillusionment and disenchantment with the present, yet it expresses a very real part of the man. For without the inspiration of such visions, Strawberry Hill would never have been built, nor would *The Catalogue of Royal Authors, The Anecdotes of Painting, The Castle of Otranto, The Mysterious Mother* and his two famous catalogue *Descriptions* of Houghton and Strawberry Hill have been written. It may even be said that because of the example of the seventeenth-century Mme de Sévigné, whom he considered his model for letter writing, he persisted in his extensive correspondence over the years. Intuitive vision, inspired by his love of the past, gave not only a significant impulse to Walpole's thought but also its coherence and structure.

That the opposition of all these forces and impulses associated with the day and night—the rational and irrational, the Classical and Romantic, the realistic living in the present and sentimental and imaginative translation into the past, the public and private—was not destructive, but, on the contrary, that it was stimulating and creative is demonstrated by the fact that because of his humanistic flexibility he succeeded in reconciling and synthesizing them throughout a long, productive, and essentially happy life. Our only conclusion must then be *not* that Horace Walpole is inconsistent, or that his contradictions were self-defeating in accordance with some preconceived logical schema arbitrarily applied to him, but, rather, that he possessed a multiple nature, versatile, complex, ambivalent, and therefore continually interesting. Hopefully, this summary and revaluation of his major accomplishments may communicate a sense of his intellectual worth and afford a real measure of the thinking man and writer.

Notes and References

Chapter One

1. In 1770 he also offered a substantial sum of money, to make up the difference, to Mme du Deffand when her pension was considerably reduced. Other instances of his warmth of feeling may be cited: his devotion to his mother, his loyalty to his father, his affection for his sister and numerous friends—Mann, Chute, Selwyn, Williams, Edgecumbe, Lady Aylesbury, Lady Ossory, Mme du Deffand, Hannah More, Mary Berry. Moreover, he took care of a natural daughter of his father until she died (Cole's Account of his Visit to Strawberry Hill, October 29—31, 1774, Yale Walpole, II, 371—73). He watched after Mrs. Leneve, the companion of his mother and sister, and was with her in her last illness. Profoundly moved by injustice, he tried hard to save Admiral Byng from execution. He did not have the heart to cashier his ignorant and inefficient old gardener who had been in his employ over twenty-five years (to Harcourt, October 18, 1777). Like William Blake, he wished to alleviate the woes of chimney cleaners (to Conway, November 28, 1784). Even his tenderness to children and animals is typical of the man's essential humanity.

2. T. B. Macaulay, "Horace Walpole," *Critical and Historical Essays* (Everyman Library, 1907), pp. 331—46. First published in 1833.

3. W. S. Lewis estimates that at present about a thousand letters in the correspondence are still to be recovered. *Horace Walpole's Library* (Cambridge, 1958), p. 65.

4. *Description of Strawberry Hill, Works* (1798), II, 404.

5. Ed. Lord Wharncliffe (London, 1866), I, 72—73.

6. In 1796 Walpole himself passed this scandalous gossip on to Joseph Farington. See Yale Walpole, XV, 324. The only reputable scholar today who presents an argument for the possible veracity of Lady Louisa and her grandmother is J. H. Plumb in his *Sir Robert Walpole: The Making of a Statesman* (London, 1956), I, 258—59. Peter Cunningham, the nineteenth-century editor of Walpole's letters, credits the story in the preface to his edition (pp. ix—x).

7. In his *Reminiscences Written in 1788* (*Works,* IV, 300), Walpole mentions Carr, Lord Hervey, along with his mother as members of the

court of the Prince and Princess of Wales. That is all. For W. S. Lewis'
negative, see *Yale Review*, XXII (1932), 211.

8. *Reminiscences, Works*, IV, 274–275.

9. *Works*, IV, 275–76. See also to Mann, February 25, 1782.

10. To Miss Berry, August 16, 1796.

11. *Memoirs of George II* (1822), I, 128–29.

12. *Description of Strawberry Hill, Works* (1798), II, 452.

13. Kenneth Clark, *The Gothic Revival* (London, 1928), p. 28;
Horace Walpole's Fugitive Verses, ed. W. S. Lewis (New York, 1931),
p. 4.

14. To Mason, May 15, 1773; to Pinkerton, June 26, 1785.

15. *Horace Walpole's Fugitive Verses*, ed. Lewis, pp. 105–6.

16. *Memoirs of George II*, I, 73. Robert, Jr., was also married, but
not happily, to the wealthiest heiress whom his father could obtain for
him, Margaret, daughter of Samuel Rolle. She brought him a substantial
dower in rents and money, and the control of the boroughs of
Callington and Ashburton.

17. *Last Journals*, ed. Doran and Steuart (London, 1910), II, 454.

18. This is Ketton-Cremer's estimate. In a letter to Conway, July 20,
1744, Walpole writes that his places brought him about £2000 a year.
Walpole himself provides figures in his "Account of My Conduct
Relative to the Places I Hold Under Government and Towards
Ministers" (1782), *Works*, IV, 364–66. W. S. Lewis, *Horace Walpole*
(New York, 1961), p. 20, says Walpole's income reached £8000 in 1784
(just before his brother Edward's death), a figure which represented
about $200,000 in the 1960's.

19. See to Montagu, September 3, 1748, for Walpole's remarks on
Gray's melancholy, frigid dignity, and disagreeable temperament.
Walpole also discussed the quarrel with John Pinkerton: see Pinkerton's
Walpoliana (London, n.d.), I, 95.

20. *Works*, I, 4–16.

21. For example, to Montagu, September 17, 1745. Conway had
also fought at Fontenoy, where the English were defeated.

22. *Works*, I, 25–27. *"Tamerlane,"* Walpole's note explains, is always
acted on the fourth and fifth of November, the anniversaries of King
William's birth and landing.

23. For example, to Mann, August 1, 1746; and to Montagu, August
16, 1746.

24. *Works*, II, 549–76.

25. *Works*, II, 560–61.

26. *Memoirs of George II* (1822), I, 35, 297, 489; II, 91, 239, 414.

27. The *Paris Journals* are in Yale Walpole, VII, 257–375.

28. The new English ambassador following Lord Hertford was the
duke of Richmond, whom Walpole also knew very well and whose

politics were very agreeable to him. Furthermore, Richmond's wife was
Henry Conway's stepdaughter.

29. Yale Walpole, III, xxxii, 46, 330, 334.
30. Lewis, Yale Walpole, III, xxxv.
31. *Horace Walpole's Fugitive Verses*, ed. Lewis, pp. 62–63.
32. Strachey, "Mme du Deffand," *Biographical Essays*, p. 184.
33. Yale Walpole, VIII, 71–73.
34. *Horace Walpole's Fugitive Verses*, ed. Lewis, p. 63; to Mme du
Deffand, October 10, 1766.
35. Repeated to Conway on June 30, 1776.
36. See *Gentleman's Magazine* (September, 1778), p. 424. Another
hostile remark appeared in the *Monthly Review* (May, 1777), a few
months before the publication of the *Miscellanies*.
37. *Gent. Mag.* (April, 1782), p. 195. See *Gent. Mag.* (April, May,
June, July, 1782); *Works*, IV, 205–45.
38. *Walpoliana*, I, xlvi.
39. *Works*, IV, 407; *Horace Walpole's Fugitive Verses*, ed. Lewis,
p. 91.
40. Also to Conway, July 2, 1795. (For more on Walpole's relations
with royalty, see to Montagu, October 14, 1760; to Lady Ossory, July
14, 1783; to Mann, May 29, 1786.)
41. But Walpole's last known letter was addressed to his niece, the
Duchess of Gloucester, February 6, 1797.

Chapter Two

1. *Works* (1798), II, 453. All references in the text will be to the
Royal Authors in the *Works* edition.
2. To Hannah More, July 25, 1790; and to Mason, March 22, 1796.
3. *Memoirs of George II* (1822), I, 327. For more on Walpole's
"republicanism," see John Pinkerton, *Walpoliana* (London, n.d.), I, 6,
91, 98.
4. Walpole also wrote *Reminiscences of the Courts of George I and
II* for the Berry sisters. See *Works* (1798), IV, 271–318. He had even
begun a journal in 1746, his first *Memoires, from the Declaration of the
War with Spain*, still unpublished. His very last journal, for the years
1783–91, also unpublished, is annotated in G. P. Judd's Yale
dissertation, 1947.
5. Gray to Walpole, December 15, 22, 1746; October 8, 1751;
Walpole to Montagu, June 6, 1752, December 23, 1759. W. S. Lewis,
Horace Walpole (New York, 1960), p. 81, says that Richard Bentley,
Mme du Deffand, and probably Conway also knew of their existence.
Ketton-Cremer, *Horace Walpole* (London, 1940), p. 127, adds Mann.
We can also add Thomas Kirgate, Walpole's secretary and printer, to
this list.

6. All references in the text are to the *Memoires* [*sic*] *of the Last Ten Years of the Reign of George II,* ed. Lord Holland (London, 1822). Walpole's spelling is modernized in our study.

7. "Detached Thoughts," *Works,* IV, 368.

8. Repeated in I, 377—78. The point is this: formerly the lord treasurer and his associates controlled the funds that were used for bribery. But George II and his grandson George III began to use the enormous monies assigned to them by Parliament for these political expenses.

9. Cf. *Last Journals,* ed. Steuart, II, 488.

10. All references are to the edition by G. F. Russell Barker (London, 1894), four vols.

11. Romney Sedgwick is also skeptical of Walpole's criticism of George III and the court. See his essay on Walpole in *From Anne to Victoria* (New York, 1937), p. 278; also Herbert Butterfield, *George III and the Historians* (New York: Macmillan, 1959). Carl Becker develops the thesis that this theory of the reign of George III is inconsistent with the ideas expressed in Walpole's own letters written between 1760 and 1772. Walpole, according to Becker, did not perceive at the time he was writing these letters any plan for increasing the prerogative, believing that the king was to be pitied for his weakness rather than feared for his strength. Becker concludes that Walpole revised the original *Memoirs* in 1775 at the beginning of the American war and thereafter, when he adopted the now traditional Whig view. "Horace Walpole's Memoirs," *American Historical Review,* XVI (1911), 255—72, 496—508. But Becker fails to note that Walpole, in at least two important works long before the American war, expressed his fears of the royal prerogative, *Royal and Noble Authors* (1758) and *Memoirs of George II.* Walpole's revisions and re-emphases simply express his settled convictions more clearly.

12. Walpole despised Johnson and always criticized him harshly: to Mason, February 7, 1782; to Lady Ossory, August 29, 1785; to Conway, October 6, 1785; "General Criticism on Dr. Johnson's Writings," *Works,* IV, 361—62; *Last Journals,* ed. Steuart, I, 444.

13. Walpole explains in a footnote how easily he could be punished for his opposition: "As Usher of the Exchequer, I advanced a very large sum of money every year to furnish the Treasury with paper, stationery wares, etc., and to pay the workmen; so that, if the payments are kept back, I am a considerable sufferer." (*Memoirs of George III,* I, 168 n.)

14. See *Memoirs of George II,* II, 239; *Memoirs of George III,* II, 139; and *ante,* pp. 24—25.

15. Cf. Namier & Brooke, *The Hist. of Parliament: The House of Commons,* III, 597.

16. Except for the fragmentary *Journal 1783—91,* still in manuscript.

17. All references are to the edition by A. F. Steuart (London, 1910).

18. According to Walpole, his brother Edward, a "most warm anti-American," became very angry at those who disapproved of the American war (II, 455); and at one point (1780) Walpole declared that the so-called independent country gentlemen in Parliament, who before had been called Tories, were as much to blame as the court for the wretched condition of the country and the violence against America (II, 264).

19. In the unpublished *Journal 1783-91* (January 13, 1784), Walpole repeated this assertion in even stronger terms.

Chapter Three

1. *Aedes, Works* (1798), II, 242, 249, 255, 256; see also *Anecdotes of Painting, Works,* III, 489. The following references to the *Aedes* are placed in the text.

2. *Vitruvius Britannicus: or, The British Architect* (1725), III, 8.

3. "On Modern Gardening," *Works,* II, 535.

4. *Works,* II, 535.

5. Plumb, *Robert Walpole,* II, 83.

6. *Works,* II, 262, 263, 242, 247.

7. *Walpole Society,* XXVI (1937–38), p. 121.

8. *Description of Strawberry Hill, Works,* II, 402.

9. *Horace Walpole's Correspondence,* ed. W. S. Lewis (New Haven, 1937), I, xxix–xxx; W. S. Lewis, *Horace Walpole's Library* (Cambridge, 1958), pp. 20–21; *Description of Strawberry Hill, Works,* II, 475; to Ibbot, September 24, 1773.

10. Hussey, *English Country Houses: Early Georgian* (Country Life, 1955), p. 72.

11. *Horace Walpole's Fugitive Verses,* ed. W. S. Lewis (New York, 1931), p. 48.

12. John Pinkerton, *Walpoliana* (London, n.d.), II, 157; *A Description of the Villa of Mr. Horace Walpole at Strawberry-Hill Near Twickenham, Works* (1798), II, 399n.

13. His total expenditure on Strawberry Hill to 1795, including land, building, and furnishing (but exclusive of the valuable collection of antiques and artifacts) amounted to well over £20,000. *Strawberry Hill Accounts,* ed. P. Toynbee (Oxford, 1927), pp. 21, 48–50.

14. *Works,* III, 94. But he disliked the Gothic poets. To Cole, March 9, 1765; to Mason, April 18, 1778; *Works,* IV, 232.

15. A painting by Canaletto, "Inside King's College Chapel," was hanging in the Waiting Room. See also *Anecdotes, Works,* III, 450.

16. The dates, occasionally differing from those given in the

Description, are taken from Lewis's "Genesis of Strawberry Hill," *Metropolitan Museum Art Studies*, V (1934), 57—92.

17. Hussey, *English Country Houses: Early Georgian* (Country Life, 1955), p. 211. (2nd ed., 1965, p. 213.)

18. *Description, Works*, II, 461; Lewis, "Genesis," p. 78; Gray to Wharton, August 5, 1763.

19. *Description*, p. 401.

20. To Cole, August 12, 1769; to J. C. Walker, December 21, 1790; and *Anecdotes, Works*, III, 99.

21. To Mann, April 27, 1753; to Bentley, September, 1753, on "the charming venerable Gothic scene" at the Oxford colleges in the dark. Walpole himself used the word "magic" in connection with Gothic in the *Anecdotes of Painting*.

22. Preface to *Description, Works*, II, 395—98.

23. To Mann, April 30, 1763. It is ironic that the home of an ardent anti-Catholic like Walpole should now be owned by the Roman Catholic Congregation of St. Vincent de Paul, and used as a normal school (St. Mary's). The interior chapel is now used for religious services. Though stripped of Walpole's furniture, all else is preserved—its fireplaces, stained glass, book cases, wallpaper, ceilings, etc.

24. Hussey, *English Country Houses*, p. 211.

25. Lewis, "Genesis," pp. 89—90.

26. A note to one of the paintings in the Gallery (*Descr.*, p. 466) explains that "the idea of the picture walking out of its frame in *The Castle of Otranto*, was suggested by this portrait"—that of "Henry Carey lord Falkland, deputy of Ireland, and father of the famous Lucius lord Falkland; in white, by Vansomer."

27. See to Mme du Deffand, January 27, 1775; W. H. Smith, *Architecture in English Fiction*, pp. 79—81, and *Times Literary Supplement*, May 23, 1936, p. 440.

28. Preface, *Description, Works*, II, 398.

29. *A Catalogue of Engravers* (1764), *Works* (1798), IV, 1—118. An important part of Walpole's history of art is included in this discussion.

30. *Walpole Society*, III (1914), 122; Katherine Esdaile, *Times Literary Supplement*, March 19, 1931, p. 224; Vertue Notebooks I, *Walpole Society*, XVIII (1930), x.

31. *Works*, III, 3. The subordinate clause is the motto of the Walpole Society. From this point, references to the *Anecdotes* are in the text.

32. Paget Toynbee, ed. "Horace Walpole's Journals of Visits to Country Seats," *Walpole Society*, XVI (1928), 9—80.

33. *Works*, III, 453—73; the quotations are from pp. 453, 454, 458.

34. *Anecdotes*, Chapter 5, *Works*, III, 92—102.

35. *Anecdotes, Volume the Fifth*, eds. F. W. Hilles and P. B. Daghlian (New Haven, 1937), pp. 158—59.

36. *Anecdotes, Works,* III, 144, 146, 430, 432, 485.
37. *Volume V,* pp. 185, 217.
38. *Works,* III, 438, 453−62; *Volume V,* pp. 60−72. The Preface includes a magnanimous estimate of Hogarth's genius; and the Advertisement of the Fourth Volume (*Works,* III, 399) contains a long note on Reynolds.
39. *Volume V,* pp. xiii, 228−40; also *Anecdotes, Works,* III, 400−01; and *Description of Strawberry Hill, Works,* II, 503−04, 511.
40. Walpole recommended the use of "gardenist" for "the projector" or "the designer of modern improvements in Landscape-gardens." *Anecdotes of Painting, Works* (1798), III, 438n.
41. To Bentley, September (?), 1753.
42. *Works,* II, 225. And in his own Bedchamber at Strawberry Hill there hung "A landscape by Mr. Taverner, exactly in the manner of Gaspar Poussin." *Description of Strawberry Hill, Works,* II, 453.
43. *The World, No. 6* (February 8, 1753), *Works,* I, 148.
44. *Anecdotes, Works,* III, 488, 490. Walpole also admired Lancelot "Capability" Brown: to Mason, February 10, 1783.
45. *Works,* III, 437−38n. See *Anecdotes, Works,* III, 434n. for another remark that explains the nature of the picturesque effect that pleased him so much.
46. To Mann, September 30, 1784; W. H. Smith, *Philological Quarterly,* XXIII (April, 1944), 180.

Chapter Four

1. Montague Summers denies that it was "the parent and source" of the historical novel (*The Gothic Quest* [London, 1936], p. 162). Yet on p. 184 he outlines the actual history of Manfred, or Manfroi, a natural son of the Emperor Frederic II, which Walpole might have known.
2. Page numbers refer to Walpole's edition, *Works* (1798), Vol. II.
3. Perhaps Jerome is an exception—cunning monks are the stock-in-trade of Gothic fiction. But Walpole does develop such figures in *The Mysterious Mother.*
4. Cf. to Jephson, November 17, 1781, on the stage version of the novel: "For effect no play ever produced more tears." Walpole's brother Edward described the romance (October 18, 1777) as "the finest portrait of melancholy that ever was drawn."
5. For Scott's comments, see Caroline Spurgeon, ed. *The Castle of Otranto* (New York, 1923), pp. xlv, xlvii. Scott also described its favorable reception in his Dedicatory Epistle to *Ivanhoe* as "a goblin tale which has thrilled through many a bosom."
6. *Walpoliana,* II, 111−12; to Lady Craven, November 27, 1786.

7. Repeated in letters to M. Elie de Beaumont, March 18, 1765; and to Joseph Warton, March 16, 1765.

8. Yale Walpole, III, 260. The original is in French.

9. In his conversations with Pinkerton, Walpole offers another version of the composition of his romance: "I wrote the 'Castle of Otranto' in eight days, or rather eight nights: for my general hours of composition are from ten o'clock at night till two in the morning." *Walpoliana,* I, 22.

10. Walpole's profound affection for Conway can be seen in numerous letters: ? 1741; October 18, 1759; February ?, 1761; July 14, 1761; April 21, 1764; June 5, 1764 (to Pitt); September 17, 1782. That of July 20, 1744, makes clear that Walpole's affection was grounded on Conway's relationship with Walpole's mother.

11. *Reminiscences Written in 1788, Works,* IV, 274–75.

12. *Walpoliana,* I, 32.

13. "Thoughts on Tragedy," *Works* (1798), II, 305–14; "Thoughts on Comedy," *Works,* II, 320; "Postscript to *The Mysterious Mother,*" *Works,* I, 128, 129; John Pinkerton, *Walpoliana,* I, 43; to Lady Craven, December 11, 1788.

14. *Works,* II, 304.

15. "Thoughts on Tragedy," *Works,* II, 307.

16. "Postscript," *Works,* I, 129.

17. *Works,* IV, 396–97.

18. Act, scene, and page references are to the *Works* edition (1798), Vol. I.

19. "Epilogue," *Works,* IV, 398.

20. *Works,* I, 128.

21. "Thoughts on Tragedy," *Works,* II, 306.

22. The relationship between Manfred and Hippolita was also considered too close according to ecclesiastical law, and they needed church sanction for their marriage! Other references to incest occur in the *Works,* I, 172–73; II, 308.

23. Cf. Ketton-Cremer, *Life of Horace Walpole* (New York, 1940), p. 282.

24. Yale Walpole, I, 46, 334, 530; see also III, xxi–xxxii.

25. See J. H. Plumb, *Sir Robert Walpole: The Making of a Statesman* (London, 1956), I, 257, n. 2.

26. *Works* (1798), IV, 321. W. S. Lewis owns a seventh, as yet unpublished, tale, and suggests that an eighth might have been written. *Horace Walpole* (New York, 1960), p. 161; Mason to Harcourt, November 20, 1788; Yale Walpole, XXIX, 333–34.

27. *Works,* IV, 322.

28. Note to Tale 1 in the 1926 edition.

29. *Works,* IV, 352.

30. A small edition in 1926 (London), limited to 250 copies, reprints the tales and includes the brief notes from Walpole's manuscript of his copy of the first edition.

31. *Works,* IV, 332. For more on Walpole's references to incest, see *ante,* p. 114 and n. 22 above.

32. Cf. Yale Walpole, XXXII, 59; *Hieroglyphic Tales* (1926), pp. 82, 83.

33. *Works,* IV, 346, 348.

Selected Bibliography

PRIMARY SOURCES

Anecdotes of Painting in England: Volume Fifth and Last. Eds. F. W. Hilles and P. B. Daghlian. New Haven: Yale University Press, 1937. Gathers additional materials dealing with Walpole's views on art.

The Castle of Otranto. Ed. Caroline Spurgeon with Walter Scott's Introduction. New York: Stokes, 1923. Valuable preface and introduction.

The Castle of Otranto and The Mysterious Mother. Ed. Montague Summers. London: Constable, 1924. Informed introductory essay, includes Mason's emendations for play.

The Castle of Otranto. Ed. Oswald Doughty. London: Scholartis, 1929. Provides excellent bibliography for Walpole and the Gothic movement.

The Castle of Otranto. Ed. W. S. Lewis. London: Oxford University Press, 1964. Interesting introduction in most recent edition.

Fugitive Verses. Ed. W. S. Lewis. London: Milford, 1931. Excellent and only edition of Walpole's poetry, all illuminating his character.

Journal 1783–91. Ed. G. P. Judd. New Haven: Yale University Press, 1947. Unpublished dissertation. The only source for this fragmentary journal. Judd's book (see below) forms the first part of this dissertation.

Last Journals . . . from 1771 to 1783. Ed. A. Francis Stewart. London: Lane, 1910. (First ed., 1859.) Part of Walpole's extensive review of English politics, important for his political views.

Letters of Horace Walpole. Ed. Mrs. Paget Toynbee. Oxford: Clarendon, 1903–5. Supplement. Ed. Paget Toynbee. 1918–25. Second most important source, next to Yale ed., for the correspondence; arranged chronologically.

Manuscript Common-Place Book. Ed. W. S. Lewis. New York: Rudge, 1927. Facsimile of materials used by Walpole in his letters; shows how serious he was as critic and collector of art.

Memoirs and Portraits. Ed. Matthew Hodgart. London: Batsford, 1963.
Useful, convenient selection of Walpole's important sketches.

Memoires of the Last Ten Years of the Reign of George II. Ed. Lord
Holland. London: Murray, 1822. Indispensable for Walpole's
political views, but unfortunately editorially censored.

Memoirs of the Reign of George the Third. Ed. G. F. R. Barker.
London: Lawrence & Bullen, 1894. Essential for Walpole's
politics, but has unacknowledged editorial censorship.

Reminiscences Written in 1788. Ed. Paget Toynbee. London: Milford,
1924. Printed in full, some passages having been omitted in the
Works edition.

Strawberry Hill Accounts. Ed. Paget Toynbee. Oxford: Clarendon,
1927. Continuous illustrated record of expenditure on the
building and furnishing of the house, and on the landscaping;
heavily annotated.

The Works of Horatio Walpole, Earl of Orford. London: Robinson &
Edwards, 1798. Five vols. First published edition, essential to any
serious study.

The Yale Edition of Horace Walpole's Correspondence. Ed. W. S. Lewis.
New Haven: Yale University Press, 1937–. Immense definitive
edition of all of Walpole's correspondence, carefully and richly
annotated and indexed; includes much material in appendices.

SECONDARY SOURCES

ALLEN, BEVERLEY S. *Tides in English Taste.* Cambridge: Harvard
University Press, 1937. Traces changes in taste for architecture,
gardening, and related arts.

BECKER, CARL. "Horace Walpole's Memoirs of the Reign of George
III," *American Historical Review,* XVI (1911), 255–72,
496–508. Discusses impact of Walpole's revisions.

BERRY, MARY. "Advertisement." *The Letters of Horace Walpole,* ed.
Joseph Wright. London: Bentley, 1840. Vol. VI. Rebuts
Macaulay.

BIRKHEAD, EDITH. *The Tale of Terror.* New York: Russell & Russell,
1963. First ed., 1921. Early discussion of the Gothic novel and its
general characteristics.

BRANDENBERG, ALICE S. "The Theme of *The Mysterious Mother,*"
Modern Language Quarterly, X (1949). 464–74. Discusses
frequent use of incest by eighteenth-century writers.

CHASE, ISABEL W. U. *Horace Walpole, Gardenist.* Princeton:
Princeton University Press, 1943. Includes a definitive edition of
Walpole's essay on gardening and places his ideas in their
historical context.

CLARK, KENNETH. *The Gothic Revival.* London: Constable, 1928. Traces neo-Gothic impulse in literature and architecture, and assesses Walpole's position and influence.

COOKE, ARTHUR L. "Some Sidelights on the Theory of the Gothic Romance," *Modern Language Quarterly,* XII (1951), 429–436. Five critical justifications for the Gothic genre.

DOBRÉE, BONAMY, "Horace Walpole." Carroll Camden, ed., *Restoration and Eighteenth Century Literature: Essays in Honor of A. D. McKillop.* Chicago: University of Chicago, 1963. Interesting attempt at psychological analysis.

DOBSON, AUSTIN. *Horace Walpole: A Memoir.* London: Osgood McIlvaine, 1890. Rev. ed. by Paget Toynbee, 1927. An elegant and graceful appreciation.

EVANS, BERTRAND. *Gothic Drama from Walpole to Shelley.* Berkeley: University of California, 1947. Indispensable pioneer study of the first fifty years of Gothic drama.

GWYNN, STEPHEN. *The Life of Horace Walpole.* Boston: Houghton Mifflin, 1932. Interesting, sometimes biased biography.

HARFST, BETSY. *Horace Walpole and the Unconscious: An Experiment in Freudian Analysis.* DeKalb: Northern Illinois University, 1968. Unpublished dissertation. Analyzes all of Walpole's imaginative works, excluding the verse.

HAZEN, ALLEN T. *A Bibliography of Horace Walpole.* New Haven: Yale University Press, 1948. Indispensable listing of Walpole's writings, their editions, and some present locations.

———. *A Bibliography of the Strawberry Hill Press.* New Haven: Yale University Press, 1942. Companion to the preceding volume; bibliographical analysis of all the publications of Walpole's private press.

HOLZKNECHT, KARL L. "Horace Walpole as Dramatist," *South Atlantic Quarterly,* XXVIII (1929), 174–89. Compares Walpole's novel and play, argues his superior skill as dramatist.

JUDD, GERRIT P. *Horace Walpole's Memoirs.* New York: Bookman Associates, 1959. Intelligent, balanced appraisal of *Memoirs.*

KALLICH, MARTIN. "Horace Walpole Against Edmund Burke: A Study in Antagonism," *Studies in Burke and His Time,* IX, Nos. 2-3 1968). 834–63, 927–45. Comprehensive analysis of Walpole's opinions about Burke and his politics.

KETTON-CREMER, R. W. *Horace Walpole.* London: Duckworth, 1940. Best comprehensive biography available.

LEWIS, W. S. *Collector's Progress.* New York: Knopf, 1951. Relates interesting personal experiences and anecdotes in his Walpoliana sleuthing.

———. "The Genesis of Strawberry Hill," *Metropolitan Museum of Art Studies,* V (June, 1934), 57–92. Illustrated account of the

construction of Walpole's celebrated suburban villa, the castle
that inspired his novel.
———. *Horace Walpole.* New York: Pantheon, 1961. Keen, appreciative
psychological and biographical study of Walpole.
———. "Horace Walpole: Antiquary," in Richard Pares and A. J. P.
Taylor, eds. *Essays Presented to Lewis Namier.* London:
Macmillan, 1956. On Walpole's antiquarian interests and
activities.
———. *Horace Walpole's Library.* Cambridge: University Press, 1958.
Delightfully informative description of Walpole's books, the use
he made of them, and of the library's dispersal.
LUCAS, F. L. *The Art of Living: Four Eighteenth Century Minds.*
London: Cassell, 1959. Includes a wise critical evaluation of
Walpole as a letter writer, critic, and friend.
MACAULAY, THOMAS B. "Horace Walpole," *Critical and Historical
Essays.* London: Dent (Everyman's Library), 1907. The famous
vituperative attack on Walpole as politician and author.
MEHROTA, K. K. *Horace Walpole and the English Novel.* Oxford:
Blackwell, 1934. Various elements in Walpole's Gothic novel and
their influence on imitators.
MEYERSTEIN, E. H. W. *A Life of Thomas Chatterton.* London:
Ingpen & Grant, 1930. Best life of Chatterton, and a defense of
Walpole's character.
NAMIER, LEWIS and JOHN BROOKE. *The History of Parliament:
The House of Commons, 1754–1790.* Oxford: University Press,
1964. Important source for details about the debates and person-
alities in Parliament, a corrective to Walpole's political remarks.
PEARSON, NORMAN. "Some neglected Aspects of Horace Walpole,"
Fortnightly Review, XCII (1909), 482–94. Excellent defense of
Walpole's character; a corrective to Macaulay's attack.
PINKERTON, JOHN. *Walpoliana.* London: Phillips, *c.* 1799. The first
life of Walpole; contains interesting anecdotes about him and his
friends.
PLUMB, J. H. *Sir Robert Walpole.* London: Cresset, 1956, 1960. Best
biography of Walpole's father.
RAILO, EINO. *The Haunted Castle: A Study of the Elements of
English Romanticism.* London: Routledge, 1927. Traces themes
of horror-romanticism beginning with Walpole's novel; argues for
extensive borrowings from Shakespeare.
ROUND, J. HORACE. "The Origin of the Walpoles," in *Family Origins
and Other Studies.* London: Constable, 1930. On the early
pedigree of the Walpole family.
SEDGWICK, ROMNEY. "Horace Walpole," in *From Anne to Victoria,*
ed. Bonamy Dobrée. New York: Scribner's, 1937. Discusses the
editorial expurgations in Walpole's letters and memoirs.

SMITH, WARREN H. *Architecture in English Fiction.* New Haven: Yale University Press, 1934. Relates Strawberry Hill to Walpole's novel.

———. "Strawberry Hill and Otranto." *Times Literary Supplement,* May 23, 1936, p. 440. Explains why Strawberry Hill and Otranto differ; identifies other models for the novel.

———. "Horace Walpole and Two Frenchwomen," in *The Age of Johnson: Essays Presented to C. B. Tinker.* New Haven: Yale University Press, 1948. On the inspiration Walpole received from Mmes de Sévigné and du Deffand

———. Ed. *Horace Walpole: Writer, Politician, and Connoisseur.* New Haven: Yale University Press, 1967. Includes some important essays on Walpole's politics and literature.

STEPHEN, LESLIE. "Horace Walpole," *Cornhill Magazine,* XXV (June 1872), 718–35. Balanced graceful evaluation of Walpole's political and historical interpretations.

STRACHEY, LYTTON. *Biographical Essay.* New York: Harcourt, Brace, 1949. Includes essays on Walpole and his letters, and on Mme du Deffand, Mary Berry, and Mlle de Lespinasse.

STUART, DOROTHY M. *Horace Walpole.* London: Macmillan, 1927. Undocumented biographical sketch with some useful insights.

SUMMERS, MONTAGUE. *The Gothic Quest: A History of the Gothic Novel.* London: Fortune, 1936. Immense survey of the Gothic novel including famous and long-forgotten ones.

TOYNBEE, PAGET. "Walpoliana," *Blackwood's Magazine,* CCXXI (1927), 454–63. Stray papers, of which accounts of a dream by Walpole and anecdotes about his father are most interesting.

VARMA, DEVENDRA P. *The Gothic Flame.* London: Barker, 1957. Indispensable survey of the Gothic novel includes best stylistic analysis of Walpole's novel to date.

WARBURTON, ELIOT. *Memoirs of Horace Walpole and His Contemporaries.* London: Colburn, 1851. First comprehensive biography of Walpole's public and private activities.

WELCHER, JEANNE K. *The Literary Opinions of Horace Walpole.* Fordham University, 1955. Unpublished dissertation. Pedantic but comprehensive and thorough, therefore important survey.

YVON, PAUL. *Horace Walpole as a Poet.* Paris: Les Presses Universitaires de France, 1924. Centers on poetic ideals, criticisms, practices; includes chapters on dramatic theory and Walpole's tragedy.

———. *Horace Walpole: La Vie d'Un Dilettante.* Paris: Les Presses Universitaires de France, 1924. Lengthy psychological and literary analysis pleasantly considers every aspect of Walpole's many-sided existence.

INDEX

(The works of Walpole are listed under his name)